Towns and Villages
OF ENGLAND

STROUD

PHILIP WALMSLEY

ALAN SUTTON PUBLISHING LIMITED

First published in the United Kingdom in 1994
Alan Sutton Publishing Ltd · Phoenix Mill · Far Thrupp
Stroud · Gloucestershire

First published in the United States of America in 1994
Alan Sutton Publishing Inc. · 83 Washington Street · Dover · NH 03820

British Library Cataloguing-in-Publication Data

A catalogue record for this book is available from the British Library.

ISBN 0-7509-0589-1

Library of Congress Cataloging-in-Publication Data applied for.

Typeset in 11/13 Bembo.
Typesetting and origination by
Alan Sutton Publishing Limited.
Printed in Great Britain by
Hartnolls Ltd, Bodmin, Cornwall.

Contents

	Acknowledgements	iv
1	How it Began	1
2	Getting There	6
3	The Heart of the Town	17
4	Top of Town	29
5	Regency Stroud and After	37
6	Victorian Stroud	49
7	Church and Chapel	61
8	Public Bodies and Public Buildings	71
9	The Twentieth Century	84
	Index	90

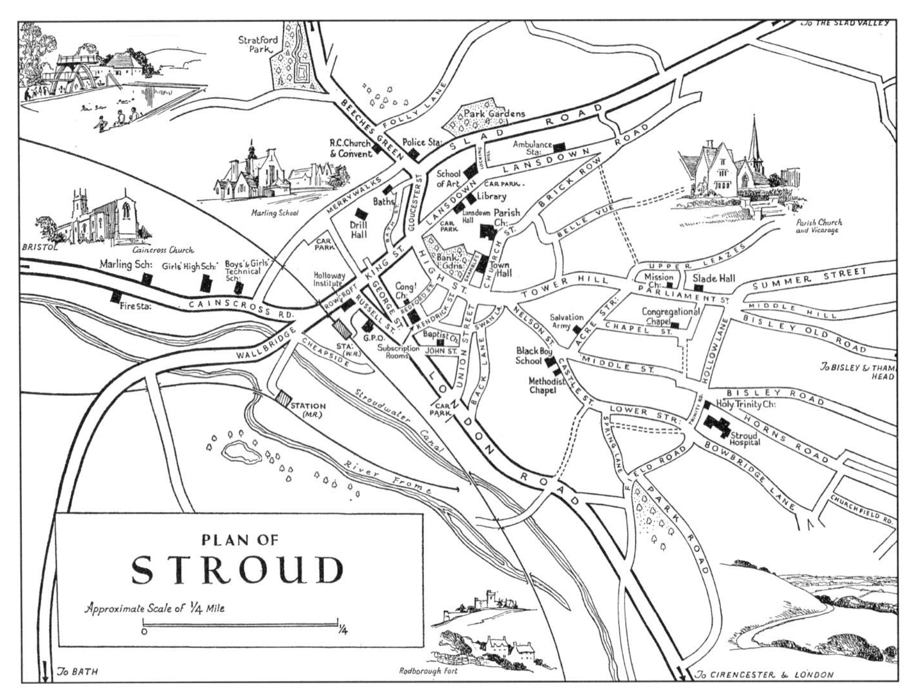

Map of Stroud, 1957 (from the Official Guide, 3rd edn).

Acknowledgements

I would like to acknowledge the help of the following in the preparation of this book:

Wilfred Merrett, Howard Beard, Stanley Gardiner, and Ann Mackintosh and the Stroud Preservation Trust for the loan of pictures; for individual illustrations, Tim Huggins (medieval building), Steve Marshfield (goods shed), Stroud District (Cowle) Museum (the Cross before 1900), Stroudwater Thames and Severn Canal Trust (Wallbridge), Peter Harris (Park's drapery store); David Smith, FSA, County Archivist and the staff of the County Record Office; the staffs of Gloucester City and Stroud Libraries; and my wife.

Philip Walmsley

Chapter One

How it Began

There are some town sites which seem to have been arranged by nature for settlements which would eventually grow into towns. Gloucester on the lowest convenient bridging-point of the Severn is one such, but it is certainly not true of Stroud.

In the Middle Ages, two great roads crossed Gloucestershire from east to west. Both set out from Cirencester, since Roman times the hub of the region's roads. The northern one passed through Bisley and Painswick before descending to the Severn at Gloucester, and the southern ran west to Minchinhampton, from there to cross the commons and descend on the south side of the valley of the river Frome, ending at one of the ancient crossing points of the Severn at Arlingham or Framilode.

By the sixteenth century both were traversing the most important cloth-manufacturing area of Gloucestershire, and the southern road was conveying bales of cloth to London to be sold at Blackwell Hall in the city.

As the industry grew the population increased, and it seemed likely that either Painswick or Minchinhampton would become the focal points of the new industry. The area between the two roads was bisected by the valley of the tiny river Frome, and the lanes which ran down from the hilltops to the mills on the stream were steep, muddy and often nearly impassable. The settlements of the area were isolated and, although the local industry depended on the mills receiving the yarn and cloth from the local villages, the lanes could often not take wheeled traffic, most movement being accomplished on foot or by donkey.

In the south-west of the largest parish in this area, that of Bisley, there had grown a small settlement at the end of the ridge between the river Frome and its Slad tributary. Along the top of the ridge ran the road to the hill-top village of Bisley, while in the other direction it crossed in turn the little Slad and Painswick streams before following the north side of the lower Frome valley towards Stonehouse and beyond.

In the later Middle Ages mills were set up on the Frome and its tributaries, and a church was built by 1279, dedicated to St Laurence, the Roman deacon reputed to have been martyred by roasting on a gridiron. The church was a so-called chapel of ease put up for the convenience of the local people and

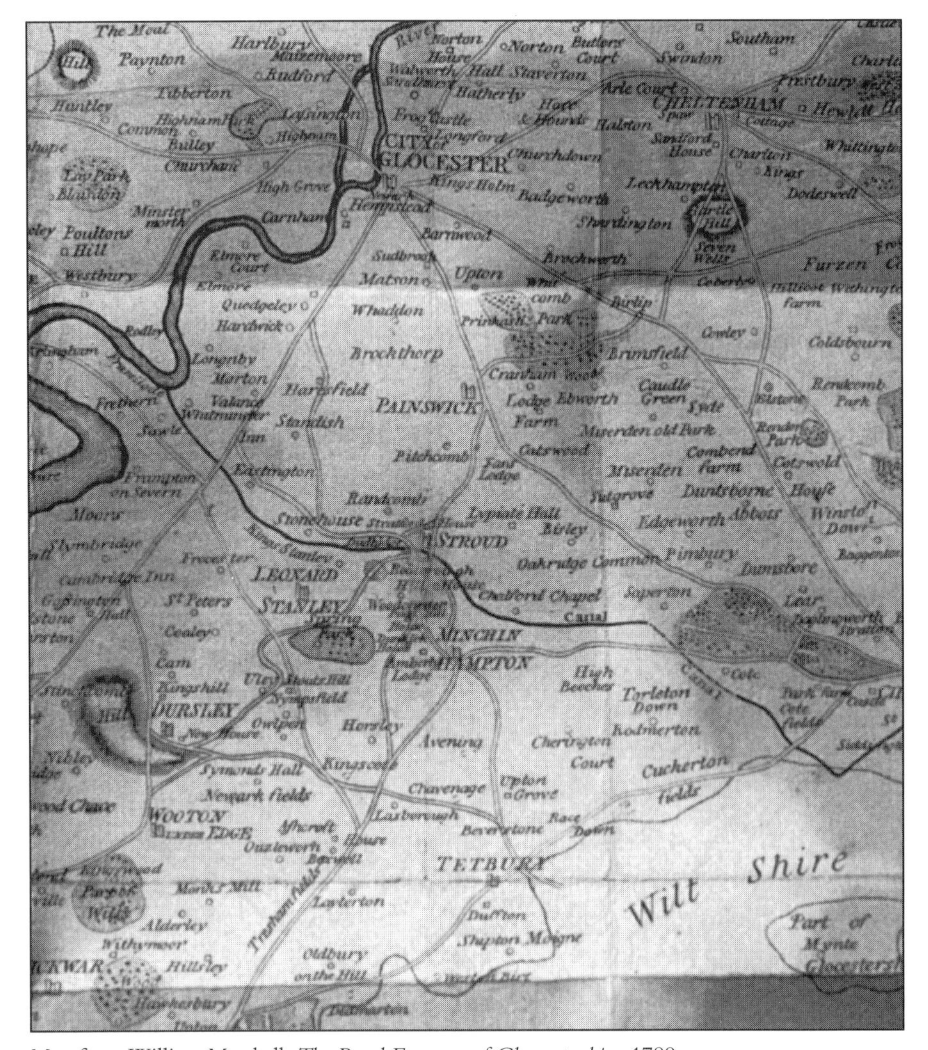

Map from William Marshall, *The Rural Economy of Gloucestershire*, 1789.

also to ensure that the mother church of Bisley obtained the dues from this remote part of the parish. Across the valley a similar development was to take place in the parish of Minchinhampton, where a church was built as a chapel of ease at Rodborough, also on the valley slope at a considerable distance from the parish church.

The Middle Ages seem to have done little more for Stroud. The manor of Bisley mentioned in Domesday Book had already been divided, and the agreement made between the rectors of Bisley and the local inhabitants

General view of Stroud, 1905.

Stroud from Beeches Green, 1930.

Windows of the medieval building discovered in High Street, 1980.

suggests that three of the smaller manors, Over and Nether Lypiatt and Paganhill, formed the parish of Stroud.

Stroud was in that part which became the Manor of Upper Lypiatt, a manor which passed through various families and in 1394 was transferred to Richard Whittington, of a Gloucestershire family and soon to be a famous lord mayor of London. The Whittingtons were to hold the manor until 1491, when it passed to their descendants, the Wyes, who held it for much of the sixteenth century.

By this time Stroud was growing as a result of the cloth trade. In 1980, as a result of demolitions for a new road, an extensive late medieval building was discovered at the top of what is now High Street. It was a large house, clearly belonging to a man of means and indicating that some inhabitants at least were prospering. With streams on three sides, there were numerous mills at work within a short distance. In them was carried out the fulling of the cloth by means of stocks (large wooden hammers powered by water-wheels), but the spinning and weaving were carried out in local cottages, and a nearby working population was needed. No village in the district can have had so many mills so near, and this surely explains why Stroud had the largest concentration of population in the area.

However, it did not yet have a market. Round it were places with grants of markets, Minchinhampton, Painswick, Bisley, both King's and Leonard Stanley, and Horsley. The Whittingtons and Wyes, living some miles away at Lypiatt, seem to have been in no hurry to have a market bestowed on Stroud, although there is mention of a market-place in the 1570s. After Thomas Wye's death in 1581, his wife married John Throckmorton, who bought the manor and soon erected a market-hall near the church. A market certainly existed in Stroud before the grant by King James I to Henry, Lord Danvers, lord of Bisley Hundred in 1607. The grant was of a market on Fridays, and two fairs on the 1 May and the 10 August, the latter the feast of St Laurence. Henry Danvers had made his mark in the world and was to make a bigger one as the founder of Oxford University Botanic Garden, but in this district he was a passing figure, who only held the lordship of the hundred for ten years before selling it in 1615. Clearly he had an eye for the main chance, knowing that market fees could make a contribution to a gentleman's income. The lords of Bisley Hundred continued to claim some income from Stroud market until the end of the eighteenth century. By the nineteenth century the dates of the fairs had been changed to 10 May and 21 August, that in May being mainly one of entertainments and in August the cattle-fair.

And so, at the beginning of the seventeenth century, Stroud was beginning to look as though it had a chance of some day outclassing its neighbours. Its church was still only a chapel of ease to Bisley, but there was now a market and market-hall. It was in the centre of a growing industrial area, and the products of that area were shortly to be of importance to both sides in the Civil War. Yet situated among the muddy lanes of the steep western Cotswold slope, its isolation was so pronounced that few might expect it to become the economic and social centre of the district.

CHAPTER TWO

Getting There

Stroud's inaccessibility was a great handicap. A map of 1720 shows no carriage road reaching it.

The town grew on what was little more than a country lane leading up a hill. At the bottom 'a deep, miry, rutty lane, between high banks' struggled up what is now Gloucester Street from a ford across the Slad stream. A narrow bridge was not built there until 1784. Half a mile up the hill, at the top of what was to become High Street, was the Cross. The lane forked there, one branch continuing up Stroud Hill to Bisley, and the other passing up and down the hillside above the river Frome until it reached Chalford.

Few travellers came this way by choice. Daniel Defoe visited the district in the reign of Queen Anne and saw two highly finished pieces of broadcloth made for presentation to the heir to the English throne and his son, the future George I and II. In his *Tour through England and Wales*, published between 1724 and 1726, he mentioned Stroud as lying in the middle of 'a most pleasant and fruitful vale . . . which is call'd Stroud-Water', but does not appear to have turned aside from the high road between Bristol and Gloucester to visit it.

Until 1752, the way to London from Stroud was up the hill to join the Painswick–Cirencester road at Bisley. In that year an act was passed authorizing a turnpike road to link the town with the road over Rodborough and Minchinhampton Commons, leading on to Minchinhampton and Cirencester. For the next sixty-three years this remained the route from Stroud to London. Beyond Rodborough Common at or near the Bear Inn were situated buildings where local cloth was collected from the whole district to be taken by carriers' carts to London to be sold.

But Stroud was now about to enjoy a drastic improvement in its communications.

Until the last century England's rivers formed an important part of the transport system, and the shocking condition of roads in the Stroud district caused some locals to consider the use of the little river Frome as a highway. In 1730 the Company of Proprietors of the Stroudwater Navigation was formed and a bill passed to make the Frome navigable from the Severn to Wallbridge below Stroud. However, the mill-owners opposed the move and nothing resulted.

Stroudwater Canal clerk's residence and office, built 1795–7.

In 1756, the scheme was revived, an alternative plan being put forward to divide the river into sections separated by locks at each mill, with loads being transferred from section to section by cranes. The purpose of this was to preserve water in each section to turn each mill's water-wheel. A new act was passed and the river course straightened in places, but nothing came of this expensive, if imaginative, scheme.

The commissioners under the two acts made a third attempt in 1774. Their plan to construct a canal parallel with the river Frome was embodied in a third act, and between 1775 and 1779 the canal was completed from Framilode on the Severn to Wallbridge.

The opening of the canal on 22 July 1779 was a splendid event in the history of the town. A booth was set up in front of the Market House in the Shambles, and the local bigwigs met to form a procession which toured the town on its way to the quay at Wallbridge. There the party embarked on a horse-drawn pleasure-boat and was pulled to Ebley Mill about a mile along the canal. On the return journey to Wallbridge it was followed by three laden

Stroudwater Canal at Ebley Mills, 1905.

barges 'freighted with Coal, Wooll, Salt and other goods', no doubt symbolic of the commodities Stroud hoped to receive in future by water.

The celebrations with which the canal was opened were justified by its commercial success. Coal dropped in price, and demand for it rose rapidly in the area.

Between 1795 and 1797, the canal company's office and clerk's house was added a few yards from the Wallbridge quay, and still stands near the Bath Road roundabout.

The Stroudwater Canal's success caused the Thames and Severn Canal Company to be launched in 1781 to extend the canal up the Frome valley and across the Cotswolds to the upper Thames, a project which, by linking England's two great rivers, was regarded as of national importance. The engineering works necessary to construct a canal through the Cotswolds greatly exceeded those demanded by the gently ascending route from the Severn to Stroud. The Stroudwater Canal had twelve locks in its eight miles, whereas the Thames and Severn had forty-seven in the nine miles which

Thames & Severn Canal at Wallbridge, 1889.

Entrance to Thames & Severn Canal Tunnel, Sapperton, 1905.

separated Stroud from the Sapperton tunnel. Moreover, the resulting canal always had problems of maintenance because of leaks and shortage of water.

From the Severn came the trows, shorter and wider than the barges from the Thames. Somewhere there had to be trans-shipment from one to the other. The Thames and Severn canal engineer, Robert Whitworth, did not choose Wallbridge for this operation, but Brimscombe, three miles above Stroud, where a port was established, an ambitious project with a basin said to be capable of holding one hundred vessels, and a large port house. As a canal port Brimscombe far outclassed Stroud.

Stroud was now a canal town. A coal depot was established at Wallbridge, and suitably named inns, the Ship and the Anchor, opened. In 1834 the Stroud Galley Company was providing weekly conveyance of goods between Bristol and Stroud, and in 1854 a trow, the *Longney*, was launched there, capable of carrying seventy tons in cargo. For nearly a century the Stroudwater Canal flourished, but after the arrival of the Midland Railway at Stroud in 1885 there was a dramatic decline in its trade.

With the success of the Stroudwater Canal the opposition of the mill-owners to opening the valleys dwindled. Sir George Onesiphorus Paul, partner in Woodchester Mill and leading local magistrate, made sure that the Nailsworth valley mills did not suffer unduly by getting a road constructed in 1780 along the valley from Dudbridge quay, one mile below Stroud, though

Brimscombe Port, 1930.

the reason he gave for building the new road was that it provided a more convenient route for those travelling between Gloucester and Bath.

The other new turnpike roads were not built until the first thirty years of the next century, after which the main roads followed the valleys. The central point of these was just below Stroud, and by 1826 five new roads led in different directions, to Gloucester, to Cheltenham, Cirencester and London, Bath and Bristol, and Stonehouse and the crossing-points on the Severn at Arlingham and Framilode.

With these thoroughfares came stage-coach services. Before 1769, there was only one weekly service to London, the Stroudwater Flying Coach. The roads after 1800 encouraged a bevy of new coaches and by 1830 there were daily services to London, Bath, Bristol, Gloucester, Cheltenham and Birmingham.

The older coaching inns, the George, the Swan and the Lamb, were situated in or near the top end of High Street, the dexterity with which coachmen negotiated the narrow streets being much admired. Paul Hawkins Fisher describes the skill with which the four-horse mail coach passed through the chicane represented by movement from Church Street across High Street into Union Street, and vice versa, the front horses trotting round the second corner before the back of the coach was round the first.

Because of this inconvenience, in 1819 Thomas Wall, the owner of the George, closed it down and took over the King's Head in King Street, renaming it the Royal George. It and the Golden Heart became the two chief inns of the town.

Stroud's roads however remained a controversial issue for many more years. The roads might be more direct, but they were often poorly maintained. The seven roads out of the town were administered by six turnpike trusts, all subject to much criticism, as the *Stroud Free Press* stated in 1851:

> Complaints are almost universal about the badness of public roads in the neighbourhood of Stroud. We are not aware of any district in the kingdom so infested with toll gates and high tolls, yet provided with such very inferior roads, while all points of egress from the town are guarded by toll-gates, often two or even three within exceedingly short distances, and the first not always clearing the second, while the tolls are by no means inconsiderable.

It was only with the creation of the county road authorities in the 1880s that the problems of the turnpike trusts were solved, and long before that a transformation in local communications had arrived with the coming of the railway.

Table of tolls at Butter Row Gate, still in position.

In 1825, because of the refusal of the Stroudwater Canal Company to reduce its charges for coal, a scheme was put forward to build a railway from the Severn to Brimscombe. It would have had horse-drawn trucks, like the tramway opened in 1811 between Gloucester and Cheltenham, but the bill authorizing it was rejected by the House of Commons.

Ten years later there were two schemes afoot to link Cheltenham, then the leading English spa, to the existing railway system. The winner was that put forward by Isambard Kingdom Brunel to provide a feeder line to the main Great Western route from Paddington to Bristol by building a line from Swindon across the Cotswolds to the Frome valley, and then taking it via Stroud and Gloucester to Cheltenham, a route which nevertheless added ten miles to the journey between London and Cheltenham compared with its rejected rival.

In 1836, an act of parliament established the Cheltenham and Great Western Union Railway Company to construct such a line. Local cloth manufacturers were among its strongest supporters, as it provided a cheaper form of transport to London for their cloth.

There were delays in the building of the railway. Seven years later, in the second edition of his poem *Stroudwater*, the local organist William Lawrence wrote:

> And we are now in constant expectation,
> That we shall someday have a Railroad Station;
> Which will, 'tis hop'd, improve the Borough trade,
> And Stroud, the central town, must take the lead;
> Then farewell horses, coaches, grooms, coach-makers,
> Inns, victualling houses, Turnpikes, and toll takers;
> For we shall fly by steam, with presto speed
> A hundred miles and no refreshment need.

In 1845 this hope was realized when, after being taken over by the Great Western Railway, the line was completed.

In its route down the Frome valley from the tunnel at Sapperton the railway ran not far from the Thames and Severn canal, which it crossed by a wooden viaduct just outside the town. The station was built in Stroud's most recent suburb, entailing the disappearance of some houses in Bath Terrace, the construction of a viaduct across the road entering the town from the south, the inconvenient lowering of the road beneath it, and the destruction of the two end houses of Rowcroft.

With the coming of the railway, the stage coaches gradually disappeared, and with them the prestige of the coaching inns. Instead of the Royal George a new railway hotel was built near the station around 1870, grandly named the Imperial Hotel.

Stroud GWR station, 1935. Brewery chimney in the background.

Stroud was also helped by the opening of the Bristol and Gloucester Railway in 1844. The nearest station on that line was at Stonehouse four miles away, but a regular horse omnibus service soon encouraged use of what was shortly to become the main Midland line from Bristol to York.

In 1849, the arrival of the railway brought Queen Victoria to Stroud, if fleetingly. In that year of cholera in London, she made her October journey from Balmoral to Osborne by avoiding the capital. This entailed changing trains in Gloucester, from the standard gauge of the Midland Railway to the broad gauge of the GWR, and then travelling to Reading. The *Gloucester Journal* grew poetic on the subject:

> Propelled by one of the Great Western's powerful eight-wheel engines, the *Warlock*, it quickened its speed every inch it advanced, flying through the Stonehouse and Stroud stations like a mass of shadow. On it rushed through the picturesque valley, up the incline, and loudly roaring, darted with a scream through the tunnel, and then burst upon the open country – Like the snow-flake on the river – One moment seen, then lost for ever.

Stroud BR Western Region station, 1950.

The arrival of the railway completely ended Stroud's isolation, and was regarded as an unmitigated blessing. In Stroud's parliamentary election of 1852, the Radical candidate John Norton became ecstatic about the influence of railways:

> Nothing has done more to develop our national greatness than our system of communication by Railways, for they have not only developed our commerce, but are increasing our comfort [and] are advancing with rapid strides our civilisation.

As the century advanced and gaps in railway coverage were filled, a branch was opened in 1867 from the Midland line at Stonehouse to Nailsworth. After the line was taken over by the Midland Railway in 1878, a short branch line was built from Dudbridge on this line to Stroud and opened to passenger traffic in 1886. Replacing the horse omnibuses which conveyed passengers to the Bristol line at Stonehouse, it encouraged the local people to use the cheap fares to the seaside resorts on the Somerset coast, and in its first years booked more passengers than the Great Western station.

However, in the history of Stroud's railway links, the climax was to arrive in the early years of the new century when in 1903 the Great Western

Imperial Hotel, Stroud, about 1910.

Interior, GWR goods shed, built 1845. Now preserved by the Stroud Preservation Trust.

inaugurated the railcar service from Chalford via Stroud to Gloucester, providing the equivalent of a tramcar service up and down the Stroud Valley, with halts at short distances along the route. This service lasted until the calamitous Beeching cuts in 1964, after which only Stroud and Stonehouse stations survived in this area.

Earlier casualties of transport changes were the canals. The Thames and Severn Canal, in spite of ownership by the County Council from 1900 and efforts to restore and revive it, was closed in two stages, in 1927 and 1933. The Stroudwater Canal, always a healthier concern, survived until after the Second World War, when it too was closed in 1954.

By this time Stroud had also returned to having one passenger station. In 1947, the Midland station was closed to passengers, and in 1966 the goods service ended. Motor transport was supreme.

CHAPTER THREE

The Heart of the Town

The difference between Stroud and most towns in southern England is the pattern of human settlement of the district in which it lies. As it grew, a belt of communities developed round it dependent on woollen manufacture. Indeed, in the seventeenth and eighteenth centuries there was less talk of the town of Stroud than there was of the district known as Stroudwater, the area round the river Frome and its tributaries which had become the principal seat of the Gloucestershire woollen industry. John Aubrey, the Wiltshire antiquarian, described its people as 'a little Commonwealth of Cloathiers and Cloathworkers – not the like in the Nation'.

Human settlement in the area had come to follow a pronounced pattern in the sixteenth and seventeenth centuries. On the streams stood the mills, with their owners' houses nearby, and on the hillsides above were the cottages of the workers, mostly weavers. The lie of the land ensured that the population did not live in lines of dwellings along lanes as in most places, but was dispersed in scattered cottages upon the hillsides.

The Gloucestershire Repository, published in Stroud in 1817, put it like this:

> The proper view to be taken of the district in question, is to consider it as a large town, the several habitations belonging to which are not, for the most part, placed side by side in rows, and front to front in streets, as is usual in cities, but are scattered throughout an extensive tract of ground, in single houses, groups of houses, hamlets, villages, and small towns; of which towns Stroud is the most considerable, and, in reference to the other parts of the district, the most centrical.

On the steep slope of Stroud Hill itself, the settlement had grown without plan. Paul Hawkins Fisher, the Stroud historian, born in 1779, remembered the town of his youth:

> Not one of the old streets was laid out in a regular form, or on a pre-arranged plan; but each house, or block of houses, was erected according to the convenience or fancy of the owner; consequently they were irregular in their lines and frontages, one house coming more forward than another,

Castle Pitch, 1900.

and all standing on the original inequalities in the surface. Moreover, the streets are generally so narrow, that not one of those above the Cross has a footpath on both sides; nor could two carriages anywhere pass one another. Besides these inconveniences, Chapel, Middle, and Lower streets range along the southern slope of the hill, and had many of the houses on their south sides several feet below the roads and the houses on their northern sides.

Between the streets and up and down the slopes ran paths, then called 'churs', a term still to be found in the chures of Stow-on-the-Wold.

Nevertheless, Stroud's High Street has always been the nucleus of the town. From the bottom it stretches in a curve up the hill until the buildings disappear out of sight. Today, the street has a sloping flat surface, but until the last century it was a hollow way with banks on either side.

To one's left is the grandest building in the street, now called Bank House, but built as a wealthy tradesman's house at the beginning of the eighteenth century. The builder was a baker called Alderley, who built in brick, making this surely the earliest brick building in the town, the brick being now covered in roughcast. According to Fisher, he obtained the bricks free from a generous brickmaker friend on the pretext that he was rebuilding the ovens of

Bottom of High Street, 1920.

Bank House, High Street, 1930, built in the early eighteenth century.

his bakery, and helped himself to enough to build the house. For some time after it was built it had the name of Alderley's Oven.

It has always been considered a desirable property. John Hollings, the earliest Stroud banker, lived there in retirement, and in 1834 it was bought by the Gloucestershire Banking Company, which installed the branch manager in the house and built banking premises next door. For many years the branch managers were members of the Winterbotham family, with whom the house has been connected until well into this century.

For a long time this family has played a prominent part in the life of the district. Its members are all descended from the Revd W.E. Winterbotham who, after being tried and imprisoned in 1793 for preaching a seditious sermon at Plymouth, was minister of Shortwood Baptist chapel, Nailsworth, between 1804 and 1829. His descendants have been solicitors, bank managers, cloth manufacturers, magistrates and chapel deacons, and one was Stroud's MP between 1867 and 1873. The name is still carried on by a law practice in the town, and was part of the name of the company, Winterbotham, Strachan and Playne, which until recently manufactured woollen cloth at Lodgemore Mill just outside the town.

In 1930, the house was bought as offices by Stroud Urban District Council, and remained as such until quite recently.

High Street is like a museum of Stroud building, though the shop fronts often conceal the date. There are seventeenth-century rubble buildings with gables on the street, smooth and classical eighteenth-century fronts, humdrum brick from the nineteenth century, and the TSB's bleak 1960s front.

Going up High Street, and passing the TSB, one comes to the part which was until 1836 the narrowest, with the front room of the Marlborough Head, later renamed the Bedford Arms, projecting nine feet into the street. Above that on market day the street became the Pig Market, with occupiers on either side of the street putting out pens for the pigs brought to market, and charging sixpence for each pen. It must have been a great nuisance, hindering passage by carriages, and leaving the street an evil-smelling mess, yet the practice continued until it was stopped by the Improvement Commission in 1825.

In the eighteenth and early nineteenth centuries not all the High Street buildings were shops. There were also houses, inns and for some time a school. On the right, on the corner of Bedford Street was Keene's workshop, a large room used at different times as theatre, Primitive Methodist chapel, and meeting-place for the local Chartists. When this workshop had been set up as a theatre in 1803, the Shakespearean actor, Edmund Kean, played there, and met an actress, Mary Chambres, whom he returned to marry at the parish church a few months later.

High Street, 1935.

There are five shops between Bedford and Kendrick Streets. The middle one, now a Wimpy bar, is on the site of Stroud's first bank, opened in 1779, and run by the partners John Hollings and James Dallaway. Stroud's first attempted bank robbery took place here, when from a cellar next door a young man named Spear tunnelled his way into the bank, and was arrested just as he broke through the floor. Eventually, he was hanged at Salisbury for an earlier crime of shooting the guard on a mail coach.

On the site of the shop at the corner of Kendrick Street was a house where at the end of the eighteenth century a Miss Jenner made a living by running both the post office and a girls' boarding school. At the times of Stroud's fairs, in May and August, she dressed her charges in white and arranged rows of seats at the windows for them to watch the fun of the fair.

Beyond this house, Kendrick Street was only opened in 1872. The building on the site of the entrance into High Street had at one time been the house of the watchmaker, John Miles, who placed on his shop the statue of the black boy holding a club to sound the hours on a bell. Since the 1840s this has been situated on the old National School in Castle Street, now used as the teachers' centre.

Opposite Kendrick Street stands one of the finest buildings in High Street, a shop now occupied by Moonflower. It was erected in 1782 by William Knight, a former London banker known locally as Banker Knight, and from 1816 to 1922 was first a druggist's and later a grocer's shop belonging to the Withey family.

It was in this building on 5 November 1824 that James Withey, High Constable of Bisley Hundred, faced the Stroud mob, enraged at the attempt to deprive them of their annual celebration of Guy Fawkes, which had previously consisted of a bonfire at the Cross and barrels of flaming pitch being launched down the High Street. No doubt with this event in mind, among the powers of the Improvement Commissioners granted by Parliament the following year was one to 'prevent nuisances in streets, or if any Person shall let off or fire any Blunderbuss, Musket, Gun, Pistol, or other Fire Arms (except in case of absolute Necessity), or shall make or cause to be made, or assist in the making of any Bonfire, or let off, fire, or throw any Cracker, Squib, Rocket, Fireball, or other Firework, or contribute or subscribe any Money or Materials for making or procuring any Bonfire or Fireworks'.

The Witheys' building was bought by the Stroud Preservation Trust in the 1980s and restored, and the considerable outbuildings at the back were turned into a complex of shops, flats and a café. A few yards further on the left, the Shambles opens out of High Street. Until 1846, the houses on either side of the opening were joined on the first floor and only a narrow entrance gave access to the Shambles.

Upper High Street, *c.* 1910.

The Shambles, 1909.

Old Town Hall, about 1870.

David Verey, in the Cotswold volume of the *Buildings of England*, calls the Shambles 'this delightful backwater', and backwater it certainly is for most of the time. All is changed on Wednesdays, Fridays and Saturdays, however, when Stroud's lively market takes over. On other days, it makes an architecturally interesting and dignified approach to the church, which indeed took over this area, Pridie's Acre, as its endowment in 1304.

The Elizabethan Old Town Hall on the right dominates the scene with its great bay window on the first floor. It began as the Market Hall when John Throckmorton, lord of Over Lypiatt manor, built it in 1594 or earlier, and only became the Town Hall in 1816–17. Now the local officials have departed, and on the ground floor it is once again primarily a market hall, with the WI market being held here each Friday morning. The first floor has been converted into a public room available for hire. It is still an attractive building, but its appearance was certainly more pleasing before the wholesale repairs of the late nineteenth century gave it vast projecting buttresses.

Opposite, the buildings formed, in succession, a house, an inn, once the Butcher's Arms and later the Corn Hall Hotel, and a corn exchange, the latter built in 1867, and later rebuilt as the parish room by the church.

From 1635 the body responsible for the Shambles and the adjacent properties built on Pridie's Acre had been the Stroud Feoffees. The stone surface of the Shambles had given the area the earlier name of the Pitching, changed in 1847 when the Feoffees paved it. At the same time they fixed the hinged butchers' stalls to the wall, and earlier they had put up the iron colonnade opposite the Town Hall.

Yet the Shambles can never have provided Stroud with sufficient room for a market. The story of Stroud's markets and fairs insofar as one can trace it is a story of changing locations.

The Friday WI market now held on the ground floor of the Old Town Hall is continuing an old story, Fisher telling us that butter women and dealers in poultry, fruit and vegetables used to resort there on market-days.

Outside, the Shambles may have begun as a general market, but it soon came to be particularly connected with butchers, who were mentioned as being there in 1630. The rest of the market was more scattered, with a concentration at the Cross at the top of the High Street.

Returning to High Street, two houses further on we come to Church

Rodney House and Parish Church, 1930.

Webb's Charity Houses, Church Street, demolished 1945.

Street, which must have been the old lane to the church, though it used to be called Lamb Lane after an inn on the right-hand side. It was always narrow, and is now a sadly decimated street, the front of the car-park occupying the site of two old houses belonging to Webb's charity which were demolished in about 1945. Thomas Webb, by his 1642 will, left his house 'over against the churchyard' and other property for charitable uses including 'the maintenance of a good schoolmaster at Stroud'. The house was later divided, part being occupied by two widows having care of the charity children and part being let. Beyond these houses was a building briefly set up as a theatre in the late eighteenth century, and later occupied as a brewery by one John Sims. Webb also built the house near the church, once 'the house behind the church' but renamed Rodney House by its nineteenth-century owner, Dr William Paine, for long the resident physician at Stroud Hospital. When owned by the clothier Robert Hughes in the eighteenth century it was reputed to have been the hiding-place at times of the robber William Crew whose sister lived there as a servant. Crew was eventually hanged at Gloucester in 1786. For most of this century it has been the vicarage, until a modern replacement was built in the grounds.

On the other side of High Street is the entrance to Union Street. In the eighteenth century this was the site of Stroud's chief inn, the George, advertised in 1812 as 'a Capital Inn for more than a Century'. A relic of it can be seen in the long flat blocked arch on the right-hand side of Union Street,

Archway of the old George, Union Street, blocked 1819.

which, Fisher tells us, led to the bar, front parlour and other parts of the inn. No doubt its congested site made it increasingly inconvenient with the multiplication of stage-coach services, and in 1819, Thomas Wall, its owner, closed it, opening the Royal George on King Street. But part of the old site became a new inn, the Swan, which still occupies this position today.

The top of the High Street is the Cross, out of which run two streets, one, now called Parliament Street, running uphill towards Bisley, and the other, Nelson Street, being the old road to Chalford. Cornhill was created about 1980 to give better access to the 'top of town'. From quite early times the Cross was the centre of the town, more of a public place than the Shambles, which was private property administered by the Stroud Feoffees. Parts of the market were held there, the corn-market until the corn exchange was built in the Shambles, and the pig-market after 1825. Fisher celebrates its many uses:

Here May-poles have been set up, adorned with ribbons and garlands of

The Cross, Stroud, before 1900.

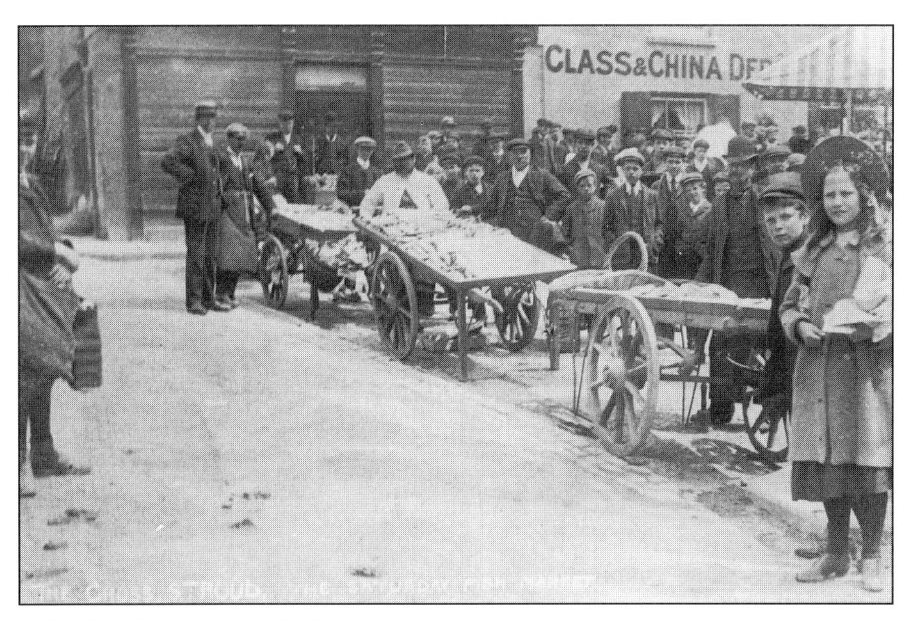

Fish stalls at the Cross, Stroud, about 1908.

> flowers, and men and women have danced round them. Here sheep and oxen have been roasted and eaten, and barrels of beer have been broached and drunk. Here multitudes have shouted for victories won, for peace restored, and other great public and local causes of rejoicing. Here, too, wild beasts are exhibited in caravans at fairs, and tamer animals are penned and sold on market days. Here the 'Cheap John' of modern times, with his wonderful volubility and sustained vociferation in selling his wares, far outdoes the mountebank and jack-pudding of old times. And, in this place as on a stage, have been acted the various businesses, the follies, and the other strange doings of many past generations.

He mentions two events of which he was a witness. In 1786, a bull was baited there, the last time such an event happened in Stroud, and in 1815 the pillory was brought from Gloucester for a local fortune-teller to be placed in it, after being found guilty of obtaining money by false pretences.

There never seems to have been a market-cross at the Cross, but in the middle was a water-pump in a small stone building, with stocks behind it where drunks were placed for punishment. There was also a room in the roof of the building called the Guard-house which was used as an overnight lock-up for criminals. The building was taken down in 1811. Later, an attempt by the Improvement Commission in 1839 to restore the old well failed because the pump provided was not strong enough to raise the water, though in 1866 a drinking fountain was set up.

The Cross is no more. In its place there is now a dull and unimaginative piece of modern townscape, the structure aptly nicknamed the 'Berlin Wall', although Jamie Vans' sculpture 'The Ram' helps to enliven it. The top of the Cross before the Co-op built its new shop in 1931 completely lacked distinction, so that the Co-op added a modest dignity now largely lost. Some time, one hopes, something will be done to make this part of Stroud more attractive and inviting.

CHAPTER FOUR

Top of Town

In his novel *The Vicar of Bulhampton* (1870) Anthony Trollope invented the Gloucestershire manufacturing town of Loring, for which Stroud is the most obvious model. They shared several of the same features, both being built on a hillside and having two churches, one up the hill and one down. But in one respect there was a great contrast. Whereas in Loring the fashionable people lived at Uphill and Lowtown was said to be vulgar, dirty and devoted to commercial and manufacturing purposes, the opposite was true of Stroud.

David Verey calls the upper part of the town 'the still extraordinarily and beautifully sited area of upper Stroud, which is full of surprises'. Such compliments were rare before this century. In 1836 the parish workhouse was reported to be in 'such an objectionable part of the town that it was recommended that no attempt should be made to render it efficient'.

Stroud grew up the hill in the seventeenth and eighteenth centuries mainly because workers settled there to work in the local industry. Hence there rose in this part of the town the usual residential units of the time, stone cottages with gabled roofs at right angles to the street. By the nineteenth century it had become a working-class suburb, with houses then built with their roof lines parallel with the street. Later, brick replaced stone for building.

Both parish and union workhouses were situated in this part of the town. Stroud parish workhouse was on the site of present-day St Alban's church, which still embodies some of its fabric. In 1724 the parish made an agreement with Thomas Poole of Minchinhampton, joiner, for the building of a workhouse, planned as a long range of two storeys with attics and sixteen bays of windows. Its inmates were employed on work connected with woollen manufacture, such as making the 'cards' (a kind of wire brush) used for preparing the wool for spinning. We are told that in 1803 the sixty-five residents earned from this employment a total of £88, about one-fifth of the cost of keeping them. The building ceased to be a workhouse in 1838 after Parliament had reorganized the poor law by combining parishes into unions. Already part of the building was being used as a school, and since then it has been employed successively as a police station, cottages and mission room before conversion into St Alban's church in 1915–16.

Further up the hill stands the big Union Workhouse opened in 1839. This was run by the Board of Guardians of the Poor, to which each parish in the Stroud Union elected members, Stroud, the largest parish, electing five.

When the Guardians first met, they had the idea of getting the medical officers to set up medical clubs in the parishes, in which families could insure against the cost of treatment and medicines by yearly payments of four shillings for a married couple and sixpence for each of their children. Unfortunately, nothing came of this precursor of the National Health Service.

The Board of Guardians' minute books still exist in the County Record Office, and from them one can learn such details as the diet of the inmates. In 1849 two and a half ounces of meat were provided for each person on Mondays and Thursdays, with eight ounces of bread for men and six ounces for women daily on other days, when meat was not provided.

The workhouse ceased to be used as such in the 1930s, was occupied by American soldiers during the Second World War, and has now been converted into flats.

Lower Street, Upper Stroud, today.

On the other side of Bisley Road is the cemetery, which came into use in 1856 because of the overcrowded state of the old burial grounds of the town. Two chapels were built, one for Anglicans and one for Nonconformists, on either side of a tower and spire, which is one of the most attractive features of this part of the town. The chapels are no longer in use and it is regrettable that suitable alternative uses have not been found for them.

Probably the oldest person buried there was Susan Dancey Face, who died in 1863 at the age of 100. An early memory of hers was of cleaning John Wesley's shoes on one of his numerous visits to the town.

This part of the town had many inns and beershops. It is recorded that an alehouse in Parliament Street bore the inscription:

All you that do this hill go up,
Pray stop and take a friendly cup,
And if you cannot drink my beer
I've other things your heart to cheer.
You can have brandy, rum or gin
And smoke a pipe if you come in.
And if you bring your horse this way
I have good stabling and good hay.

Nelson Street, 1910, the Cross in the distance.

Nelson Street is one of the most varied of the streets. It was once narrow, with high banks on the north side. Most of its houses were bigger than those higher up the hill.

There was the Knapp, which had belonged to the Revd William Johns, curate of Stroud from 1688 to 1722. In accordance with his will, after the deaths of his descendants the rent of the property was to be used for various purposes useful to the town, including annual grants to the charity schools which he had founded, and payments to tradesmen for taking on apprentices. The house became the Horse Shoes Inn, and later the New George. It has been suggested that the young James Wolfe, who was to die heroically three years later as the conqueror of Quebec, stayed in this inn when stationed in Stroud in 1756 and engaged on the task of suppressing the local weavers' strike, but it seems more likely that his quarters were in the High Street George. In 1860 the New George consisted of three properties, which were then sold by the trustees, at which time it ceased to be an inn. The cottages were finally demolished in 1963 to make way for the present car-park.

Further up the street stood the eighteenth-century Godolphin House, also

Old Bisley Road about 1910.

demolished in 1963. This was probably the house mentioned in the later eighteenth century as a school run by a Mrs Romieu. In 1779, while performing at Stroud, the actress Sarah Siddons stayed there. She was then aged twenty-four, and was described as possessing quiet and domestic habits.

In one of the cottages of Middle Street was born in 1718 John Canton, who became a distinguished scientist. His father was a weaver, and as a child he worked as a weaver's boy. He was sent to London at the age of eighteen, where at first he taught. He became a Fellow of the Royal Society in 1749, and among his many achievements he devised an instrument to measure electricity.

In the 1870s many of the older stone houses in this street were replaced by brick, largely at the expense of the owner of Lypiatt Manor, Sir John Dorington, who for a time hoped to become Stroud's MP, and achieved this ambition for twenty-eight days in 1874 (see p. 51).

At the end of the street is the terrace of Whitehall, built on the edge of the town as residences in a healthy situation for successful tradesmen. The oldest part of it is seventeenth century, and it was added to in the following centuries.

The most imposing house at the top of the town is the Castle. The oldest part is apparently early seventeenth century, but in appearance it is a handsome stone eighteenth-century house, with its claims to castle status

Middle Street, Stroud, 1910. On the left, brick houses built about 1870; on the right, earlier stone houses.

Paul Hawkins Fisher, 1779–1873.

Holy Trinity Church and Hospital, 1900.

Horns Road about 1910.

resting on the two small towers in the garden wall on the street front, though its name dates from long before they were built. From 1809 until 1873 it was the home of Stroud's historian, Paul Hawkins Fisher, solicitor, who contributed a series of articles entitled 'Reminiscences of Stroud and its Vicinity' to the *Stroud Journal* between 1860 and 1865. In 1871, at the age of 92, he published the volume *Notes and Recollections of Stroud* based on these articles, and a second edition was brought out in 1891, eighteen years after his death, with footnotes by his son. The town is fortunate to have had its years of greatest change chronicled by so lively a writer, fascinated both by the documents casting light on the remote history of the town, and also by the gossip of his own day.

This part of the town was not exclusively residential. Cottages stood next door to small industrial establishments, as the presence of Piccadilly Mill between Middle and Lower Streets still reminds us.

Stroud had once ended beyond Whitehall with the well-named Hollow Lane, which Fisher describes as being both narrow and deep in his young days, lying as it did below the level of the fields. In the early eighteenth century the open fields beyond had stretched much of the way to Bisley but had been enclosed by 1725, though there is no record of the transaction.

The nineteenth century saw more houses being built for workers in the local industry. These ribbon developments formed the built-up area along the Bisley

View of Horns valley, 1905. Workhouse and Cemetery Chapel in the distance.

Road and the lane leading down obliquely to the Slad valley, where a house called Somers gave its name to the street, a name which soon became Summer Street.

On the other side of Bisley Road building was already taking place beyond Trinity church. Much of this land was part of the Field estate which had belonged to the old clothier family of the Arundells, who died out early in the nineteenth century. In 1873, it came into the hands of William Cowle, who set about developing his property, laying out new roads and building houses for the middle classes.

One of his first actions was to offer an acre of land near Trinity Church for the building of a hospital, which was opened in 1875. On the other side of the church Horns Road was laid out leading to a suburb of houses built by the Stroud clothing manufacturer, politician and philanthropist, George Holloway, and available for purchase by their working-class occupiers.

Beyond these brick houses lies the Horns valley, once so well loved by Paul Hawkins Fisher. In his book he describes the nostalgic walk he took in the summer of 1868 at the age of eighty-nine. In fact, there has been little further development of Stroud in this direction, and well over a century later he would have recognized the features of the same walk.

CHAPTER FIVE

Regency Stroud and After

Until the end of the eighteenth century Stroud had expanded mainly up the hill. The valleys round three sides of it were left with muddy tracks leading to the mills. However, the building of the canals and the coming of the new turnpikes opened up the valleys, and in the nineteenth century Stroud expanded downhill.

The first stage began before 1800 with the building of the first houses in Rowcroft and continued until about 1840, when its end coincided with the great depression which affected much, but not all, of the local cloth industry.

The building of the turnpike roads after 1800 may have brought about improvements in Stroud streets. King Street had long existed as the first part of the lane to Wallbridge, but the creation of the Birdlip to Lightpill turnpike in 1800 made it an important thoroughfare, part of the route which at that time connected the fading spa, Bath, with the rising spa, Cheltenham. It was no wonder that Thomas Wall in 1818 decided to transfer from the George at the top of the High Street to the existing King's Arms in King Street, renaming it the Royal George, and clearly intending it to be the leading inn in the town.

On 14 August 1788, while recuperating at Cheltenham after his first mental breakdown, George III had passed through Stroud en route to visit a cloth mill at Woodchester. He rode on horseback into the town from Badbrook, accompanied in carriages by his wife, Queen Charlotte, and their three eldest daughters. Large crowds gave him a loyal welcome and noticed that he had a long tear in his coat under one arm.

On King Street, from the corner of Gloucester Street to the Royal George, there were four inns. At the corner was the Chequers, its sign a chequered square like a chessboard, and managed for eighty years by members of the Purcell family.

Next door stood the Golden Heart, an old coaching inn with many of the buildings and much of the land behind attached to it. The land included a stretch of grass called the Bowling-Green, used in many ways for over a century. In 1739, the Gloucester-born evangelist George Whitefield recorded in his journal that he preached there to an audience of several thousand. One hundred years later two Chartist speakers, Henry Vincent and W.G. Burns, spoke to a crowd at the same place, ferociously attacking Stroud's MP, the Home Secretary, Lord John Russell. In its report, the *Gloucester Journal* commented on their shabby clothes, describing them as wearing 'dark dirty-looking mackintosh cloaks and common filthy-looking travelling caps'. At the time of Stroud's August fair, the sheep market was held there.

Beyond the Golden Heart was the Green Dragon, less successful than its neighbour judging by its rapid succession of licensees in the nineteenth century.

At the end of the block stood the Royal George, in the great age of coaching the principal inn of the town. Originally on the site there had been stables and a warehouse belonging to the carrier Daniel Ballard, and it was his successor, Thomas Gardner, also a carrier, who turned it into an inn, the King's Arms, in 1801.

Seventeen years later, it became the Royal George Hotel, and was much enlarged and improved. In fact, it became a town institution, with the highly respected Wakefield family in charge from 1836 until 1853. In 1845, Mrs Mary Wakefield, the landlady, was given a public dinner at her house by the 'most respectable and influential gentlemen of the neighbourhood', including W.H. Stanton, one of the town's two MPs. It

High Street – King Street Corner, 1900.

King Street, in the 1930s.

George Hotel and King Street, 1920.

was probably at this inn that the young Charles Dickens stayed when, as a reporter, he covered for the *Morning Chronicle* Lord John Russell's first election as MP in 1835.

Like many such places, with the coming of the railway in 1845 it fell upon hard days, eventually having its first floor converted into a cinema. It was demolished in the 1930s.

On the other side of the street, at the corner with High Street, from the 1820s to the 1860s were the premises of Benjamin Bucknall, printer, stationer and bookseller. The Bucknall family was prominent in the town during much of the nineteenth century. Another Benjamin Bucknall (1833–95) was a distinguished architect who took over the plans of A.W.N. Pugin for the local country house, Woodchester Park, and adapted them to build what has been described as one of the great achievements of nineteenth-century domestic architecture in England. Woodchester Park was never completed and is now looked after by the Woodchester Mansion Trust.

The older Benjamin Bucknall is associated with the first Stroud newspaper. Until 1848 Stroud news appeared intermittently in the *Gloucester Journal*. Briefly, in 1817 and again in 1821–2, there had appeared either as a fortnightly or a monthly *The Gloucestershire Repository*, collections of articles and poems, in which Paul Hawkins Fisher, the future historian of the town, first appeared as a writer.

In 1848, the four-page *Monthly Observer* was launched by Bucknall, with his son as the editor. Unfortunately, in those days of newspaper stamps it quickly fell foul of the authorities and no copies seem to have survived. In 1850, Bucknall launched the *Stroud Free Press* as a four-page weekly. It was followed four years later by the arrival of a second weekly, the *Stroud Journal*, produced by another Stroud bookseller and printer, F.W. Harmer. With its eight pages, double the number of the *Free Press*, it killed off its competitor in 1856.

The third and fourth houses in King Street were connected with one of the most celebrated of Stroud stories, the shooting of Lieutenant Delmont in a duel in 1807.

With the Napoleonic War at its height and the Peninsular War about to begin, there were stationed in Stroud a number of recruiting officers from various regiments. The area, with its comparatively dense population and fluctuating industry, produced large numbers of recruits for the army. However, one can imagine that the recruiting officers often found time lying heavily on their hands in the course of a spell of undemanding service.

Two of the officers in the town in 1807 were Lieutenants Benjamin Heazle and Joseph Francis Delmont, of the 82nd and the 3rd Regiments respectively. During a summer afternoon's walk outside the town, Heazle objected to a

Victoria Buildings, George Hotel and King Street Parade, 1920s.

Russell Street, 1925.

remark made by Delmont, and challenged him to a duel to take place that evening. Delmont procured a second, another recruiting officer, Lieutenant Sergeaunt, who with some difficulty got a couple of pistols, and also made arrangements for a surgeon to attend.

In the evening, the three men walked to a quiet field outside the town near the Grange, a house between the Slad and Painswick streams, only Sergeaunt wearing his uniform, the others being in civilian dress, no doubt to avoid attention.

The details of the duel seem clear. Only Heazle fired, his bullet passing through Delmont's body from behind, indicating that the shot had been fired before Delmont had turned to face his opponent.

As soon as Delmont fell, Heazle and Sergeaunt left the scene. Sergeaunt obtained assistance from the Grange, after which he changed out of his uniform and left for London. On arriving there he called on Delmont's father to tell him what had happened to his son and then disappeared.

On leaving the scene, Heazle had met the surgeon making his way there and told him what had happened. He then quickly made off, supposedly following the towpath of the Thames and Severn Canal towards London.

Delmont, having been carried back to his lodging in a hand-barrow, died there four days later. The next day, an inquest pronounced a verdict of wilful murder against Heazle and Sergeaunt, but neither was ever brought to court. Delmont was buried under a flat stone in St Laurence's churchyard, with a simple inscription. In accordance with an old law, not abolished until 1846, Heazle's pistol, as the instrument of death, was forfeited as what was called a deodand. It became the property of the lord of the manor of Painswick, because the crime had been committed in that parish.

Beyond the Royal George there was an open space, and beyond that Rowcroft House, built in 1795 by Edward Thornton, later surgeon of the Loyal Stroud Volunteers. It remained a doctor's house until sold to the County of Gloucester Banking Company in 1859, after which the house was used as a bank until demolished in the 1920s to make way for the present Lloyds Bank.

With the road down to Wallbridge soon to be improved by the building of the Birdlip to Lightpill turnpike, frontages on the new road offered promising places for new development.

The handsome terrace in Rowcroft looks today as though it was built all at one time, but in fact it arrived in stages. The Stroud entrepreneur, Joseph Grazebrook, who had played so large a part in the construction of the Stroudwater Canal, built the first four houses in two blocks in 1801, siting the bank in which he was a partner in the bottom house. A few years later the space in between these two blocks was filled in by the speculative builder,

Charles Harrison, who was to carry out much of Stroud's building at this time. Further houses were also added to the upper end.

Until the coming of the railway Rowcroft was regarded as one of the most desirable locations in the town. In 1820, for example, two of the houses were a bank and an academy for young ladies, while others were occupied by a doctor, a surgeon, a solicitor and a silversmith.

Opposite the Royal George, towards the end of the eighteenth century, there stood the house and warehouses of the clothier Charles Freebury, whose land, known as Freebury's Orchard, stretched up the hill behind his house. After his death in 1795, the property passed to his nephew, Charles Kendrick, and the area became known as Kendrick's Orchard.

The development of this area followed the building in 1815 of the turnpike road along the valley to Chalford and beyond, fifteen years after the opening of the turnpike between Lightpill and Birdlip, which ran at right angles along King Street. The Stroud end of the Chalford road started opposite Rowcroft House and became Russell Street. In fact, this name was used before Lord John Russell became Stroud's MP in 1835 because of the part he had played in the passing of the Reform Act in 1832, a universally popular measure in Stroud, which had given it two representatives in the House of Commons.

George Street, 1910. On the left, the Wilts and Dorset Bank, now NatWest.

At about this time, a short street was also made from the Royal George to the new road, bearing the name of Great George Street.

Charles Kendrick died in 1818, and his son Charles Freebury Kendrick sought to make money by selling off plots of the remaining orchard. Unfortunately, this did not prevent his bankruptcy in 1832, and he and his family emigrated to America three years later.

Meanwhile, on the other side of Russell Street, the area called the Shurmers was also being developed. Charles Hodges built a house called Wellington Place, and nearer Rowcroft a new street was laid out at right angles to Russell Street, beginning as Bath Terrace and leading to Bath Place. The houses here were not as grand as those in Rowcroft, but provided residences for the town's shopkeepers and tradesmen.

Other houses soon began to appear on the new Chalford road. Victory Terrace no doubt commemorated the 1815 victory over France. Beyond it was a public house, the Sun-dial, now a private house, but still possessing the dial giving it its name.

As Stroud grew, one senses an increase in civic pride. In 1817, the *Gloucestershire Repository* had commented on the town's lack of 'common rendezvous', complaining 'we have no corporation, no exchange, no public coffee-room'.

London Road, 1905.

The Sun Dial, London Road, which is still visible.

Yet already in 1815, Joseph Birt, the owner of the White Hart at the Cross added to his inn a large room for public meetings. It was much used in the following years, and remembered by later generations for the intense debates on slavery which had taken place there in 1831–2 just before the act was passed abolishing slavery in the British Empire.

The same years saw the great national movement for the passing of the Reform Bill, an agitation in which Stroud led the county. In 1831, Richard Parker, the owner of the Royal George, must have thought that he was making a good investment when he erected the Victoria Rooms on part of the open space in front of his inn. At that time the princess Victoria was heiress to the throne, and this building was one of the first in the country to be given her name. Unfortunately for Mr Parker, the Subscription Rooms were opened only two years later and took away many of the bookings which he hoped for. Although the Victoria Rooms remained standing until the 1960s and even now a small part remains as Timpson's shoe-shop, for most of its life it had been occupied by a furniture store and shops. Nevertheless, at a time when voting in elections was still public, for many years it was in front of the Victoria Rooms that the hustings were set up for electors to cast their votes.

This was the scene of Stroud's election riot of 1834. Stroud had become

Subscription Rooms and George Street, 1910.

a two-member borough constituency under the 1832 Reform Act, and many of its residents also enjoyed votes in the county constituency of East Gloucestershire. It was a by-election for that seat which gave rise to the riot. In the 1832 election the Yellows (the local name for the Whigs) had won both the East Gloucestershire seats, chiefly because of the overwhelming support of Stroud and Cheltenham, and the Blues (Tories) now thought they had a good chance of winning the seat. Their committee room in Stroud was the Royal George next to the hustings, but on the first of the two election days, 11 and 12 August, the Yellow mob put the inn under siege, and so it remained during the whole two days, attempts to restore order by magistrates and local constables proving quite ineffective. By the time that voting ended, all the inn's windows and doors had been destroyed. Compensation was paid later by the Hundred of Bisley, but only four rioters were prosecuted and found guilty. When the votes were counted, the Tory candidate, C.W. Codrington of Dodington Park, was found to have a majority of seventy.

Stroud in the 1830s prided itself on its progress. As the Tory *Gloucestershire Chronicle* reported in 1834,

> In addition to our New Rooms, new Casualty Hospital, intended new Schools, and threatened new Meeting-house, we are to have a new Bank, and a new Water Company.

One might add to these amenities the lighting of the town by gas in 1833.

This phase in the town's history was shortly to come to an end. The local industry of woollen cloth manufacture was always subject to ups and downs in its prosperity, and the worst of these was to arrive in 1837, when many mills went out of business and their owners were bankrupted. There was some slight recovery in the 1840s and the arrival of the railway in 1845 certainly gave new life to the local economy, although it also set limits on the town's physical expansion.

Stroud Brewery was sited between Rowcroft and Wallbridge after being moved from Middle Lypiatt in 1793. Its first years at the new site were not easy judging from the following advertisement in the *Gloucester Journal* in 1799:

> TWENTY GUINEAS REWARD
>
> The Counting House at the Brewery, in Stroud, belonging to Messrs. Leversage & Grazebrook, was between six in the evening of Wednesday the 10 and three in the morning of Thursday the 11 feloniously broken open, and one shilling and sixpence in halfpence, the current coin of the Kingdom, STOLEN therefrom. Whoever will discover the Offender or Offenders, shall, on his, her or their Conviction, receive the above award.

It was at first owned by partners, but from 1818 to his death in 1855 it was run by Joseph Watts of Stratford House, known as 'Old Joe Watts' to the Berkeley family of Berkeley Castle who cultivated him because of his political influence in the county. At one time it was said that he could get anyone he chose elected for Stroud. Almost every day he was present in his little brewery counting-house, where he met the high and mighty as well as ordinary acquaintances.

In 1888 the brewery became a limited company, and the following year new offices were built. At that time there were several other breweries in the town and district, most of which were absorbed by Stroud Brewery Company from 1897 onwards, one of the last being Godsell's Brewery at Salmon Springs on Painswick Road, where a large bottling plant was installed. As beer came to be supplied over a wider area, Stroud Ales became Cotswold Ales.

Brewery Offices, 1911, decorated for George V's coronation.

In 1962, three years after combining with Cheltenham Brewery, it was taken over by Whitbread's, and brewing ceased in the town in 1967. At the end of its life the brewery's output was 2,000 barrels a week, and it was employing over 300 people.

CHAPTER SIX

Victorian Stroud

It would be unfair to say that Stroud stagnated in the twenty years after 1840, for these were the years when the railway arrived and new industries came to the district to occupy the old mill sites, but the energies of the locals did not find an outlet in building.

Then from the 1860s onwards the urge to expand and develop once more affected the leaders of the town, and new streets were laid out and new buildings put up. The differences between this later development and the first period of expansion are plain to see in that Cotswold stone was the preferred material earlier in the century, while later a combination of brick and stone, sometimes with terracotta embellishments, was favoured. The face of modern Stroud is largely the product of these two major periods of construction.

By 1860, a new generation had arrived on the scene. Foremost in it was George Holloway, born in Hampshire in 1825. He is said by a family tradition to have arrived penniless in Stroud and to have first made a living by selling bootlaces. In 1849, with his brother Henry, he opened a clothing shop in High Street. The two brothers early saw the possibilities of Isaac Singer's invention of the first practical sewing-machine in 1851. They took over premises in the lane soon to be known as Threadneedle Street, and began to make various kinds of clothing. The manufacture soon outgrew these premises, and much of the work came to be done by local women in their homes, using machines provided by Holloway's. In a short time the manufacture of ready-made clothing became the town's leading industry.

George Holloway had other interests, which included friendly societies, working-class housing, agriculture and Conservative politics. Benefit societies had long existed in the district, their success depending on their members' ability to keep up their payments. For a small weekly payment the society paid out a weekly sum in time of illness, and at the end of the year the balance held by the society was paid back to its members.

Holloway proposed for his society that it should keep the balance and credit it to each member as the basis of an annuity to be enjoyed in old age. In 1875 the Stroud Working-Men's Conservative Friendly Society was duly launched with forty members, the first of them being Holloway. Although the society remained limited to this district, where it quickly gained and

Clothing factory, decorated for Christmas, about 1910.

retained much local support, it was widely copied elsewhere. Another similar society, the Mutual Provident Benefit Society, was also launched in Stroud, supported at first mainly by local Liberals.

In 1883, Holloway founded the Cottage Building Society to enable members of the working classes to own their own houses, and he built many houses for them in upper Stroud. Also, to promote farming co-operatives he bought a large estate near Temple Guiting, and let it out to small-holders.

He was also interested in cricket and, in his early Stroud years, had joined the town's early morning cricket club, which played the game on the common near Rodborough Fort between 4 and 7 a.m. Towards the end of his life he was the president of many local cricket clubs.

Since 1832, when Stroud became a two-member parliamentary borough, it had always sent Liberal MPs to parliament. George Holloway and his ally John Dorington of Lypiatt Park worked hard to end this situation. In 1867, they helped launch the *Stroud News*, the Conservative weekly to compete with the Liberal *Stroud Journal*. In the same year, after the passing of the Second Reform Act which granted the vote to all male householders over the age of 21, it soon became clear that the increased number of electors was more evenly divided between the parties than in the past, and so there followed a period of intense political rivalry between the two main parties.

The five elections which took place in Stroud between January 1874 and February 1875 must form a national record. In the first, in January 1874, the Conservative Dorington defeated the Liberal Sir Henry Havelock, Bt.,VC, a hero of the Indian Mutiny of 1858, in which his father had been a leading commander, and who is still commemorated in the name of a terrace on London Road. This unprecedented defeat for the Liberals played its part in persuading the Prime Minister, Gladstone, to call the general election which took place a few weeks later. In that election, W.J. Stanton and S.S. Dickinson, both Liberals, were returned, but the Conservatives petitioned successfully against the result on the grounds of corruption, and the election had to be reheld.

The third election, in May 1874, resulted in the return of the Conservative, Dorington, and the Liberal, A.J. Stanton, the brother of W.J. Stanton. The defeated Conservative candidate was George Holloway. After this election, both parties petitioned against corrupt practices by the other party. The Liberal petition succeeded, but the Conservative one failed. A.J. Stanton kept his seat, and a further election was held to replace Dorington.

Lansdown, 1910.

The Liberal candidate, H.R. Brand, won the fourth election, in July 1874, but again the Conservatives petitioned on the grounds of corruption, this time successfully. In February 1875 the fifth election in this extraordinary sequence of events took place, an election won for the Liberals by the cloth manufacturer, S.S. Marling. The final outcome was therefore the holding of both seats by the Liberals for the remainder of the life of the parliament.

George Holloway had played a leading role in these events. He stood, again unsuccessfully, as Conservative candidate in the 1880 general election, the last of Stroud's elections as a parliamentary borough. The 1885 Redistribution Act placed the old borough constituency in the new constituency of Mid-Gloucestershire, which also included Dursley and Wotton-under-Edge. In the first election for the new seat in 1885 Holloway again lost, but in 1886 the town which had made his fortune was at last represented by him in parliament. He sat for it until shortly before his death in 1892.

The Holloway brothers did not initiate the building projects which took place in Stroud in the 1860s. In 1857 John Libby and Hugh Pearce formed a partnership as cloth merchants, their early success leading them twelve years later to build an imposing cloth hall near the Subscription Rooms.

After this, the Holloways seem to have been the driving force in opening a new street from the cloth hall along the side of the Subscription Rooms to the High Street. As it was partly on the site of Kendrick's Orchard, it took

A group outside the *Journal* office, Lansdown, 1920s.

the name of Kendrick Street, and created not only a useful link between the top of the High Street and London Road, but also gave better access to Holloways' factory in Threadneedle Street. On the east side of Kendrick Street the Holloways put up an impressive line of shops, the lower ones of Bath stone, and others of brick with terracotta facings.

The cloth hall was not a lasting success and was later bought by the Holloways, who owned a great deal of this part of the town. In the same block as the former cloth hall were the office and printing-works of the new Conservative paper, the *Stroud News*.

Earlier in the 1860s, other developments were carried out by Holloway's political opponents.

Sebastian Stewart Dickinson had laid the basis of his fortune as a barrister in Bombay, and on his return to this country bought the house of Brownshill Court near Pitchcombe. In 1856 he married one of the daughters of W.H. Hyett of Painswick House, former MP for the borough, and began to nourish political ambitions himself. As with the Conservatives Dorington and Holloway his property development in Stroud may have been connected with these ambitions.

In the 1860s, he bought the Golden Heart in King Street and converted it into premises for the Stroud Mutual Improvement Society, a body of which he was president. The society rooms were equipped with a library, and reading, lecture, coffee and refreshment rooms, while Dickinson paid for the addition of a large covered skittle-alley and gymnasium, and had the old bowling-green behind relaid.

Later, he acquired property in Badbrook Lane, once a byword for its steepness and inconvenience, closed and demolished the old Chequers Inn at the top corner, and built a line of tall brick shops down the hill, after which the lane was renamed Gloucester Street. In 1868, Dickinson was elected MP for the borough.

For some time there had been pressure to build swimming baths in Stroud, and in 1869 they were opened, a rare example of political co-operation at this time as Dickinson gave the land near Gloucester Street and Holloway subscribed an equivalent sum of money. The baths were to remain in use until the Second World War.

Already from the bottom of High Street, there was a path leading down to Little Mill on the Slad stream. In a map of 1835, it was shown as a proposed road across land belonging to William Hopson, but in fact all that seems to have been done at that time was the construction of a new vicarage on the site of the present library.

By the 1860s much of this area was in the hands of Dr William Henry Paine and Edward Mansfield, and they created the new road running down to

Slad Road, 1920.

Beeches Green, 1925, the Magistrates' Court on the right.

Little Mill. If the earlier history of Stroud is written in the buildings of High Street and the Shambles, its history in the later nineteenth century is written in Lansdown.

The first new buildings were a row of brick houses, one of which became the office of the Liberal *Stroud Journal* in 1868, and is now the headquarters of the *Stroud News and Journal,* the weekly resulting from the amalgamation of Stroud's two papers in 1957. No doubt the opening of this office was the reply to the launch of the Conservative *Stroud News* the year before.

A local curate had founded Stroud Grammar School in 1871, and built the Gothic building opposite the *Stroud Journal* office to house it. The new school had a short life, though later the building was occupied by the Stroud Borough School, a more successful enterprise which ultimately had about 120 pupils. However, the building was sold to a local group wanting to commemorate Queen Victoria's Golden Jubilee in 1887 by the establishment of a Free Library, and the building was bought and adapted for this purpose.

For the first few years it was maintained by private subscriptions, but in 1897 the young Stroud Urban District Council took it over. At times it was to find its maintenance a struggle, and in 1930 it was voluntarily transferred by the UDC to the county council, which built the new library alongside in 1976.

Unitarian chapels existed in Gloucester, Cheltenham and Cirencester, and in 1876 one was built in Lansdown, but it attracted little support. It was later used in turn as Baptist chapel, Liberal hall, cinema and dance hall.

On the other side of the Old Library stands the substantial bulk of the Lansdown Hall. This was originally built as a temperance hall in 1879 largely with funds received from a legacy. For a long time temperance was one of the strongest causes in the town, the earliest temperance society in the county being founded here in 1834. A strong local supporter was Samuel Bowly, a Quaker cheese-merchant living at Edge, where each year a great temperance fête was held. He died in 1884. In the course of its history the hall has been used for many purposes, most recently as a meeting-place by Christian Scientists.

The success of the Holloways and the work it gave to the local population brought to Stroud some of the Jewish immigrants from Eastern Europe, at this time settling in much greater numbers in the East End of London, Manchester and Leeds. In Stroud there were enough Jews to found a synagogue, at first on the road to Slad, and in 1889 in Lansdown. It was used almost until the First World War, and is now a carpet shop.

George Holloway was responsible for another addition to Lansdown, the creation of a cattle market at its far end in 1889. But his aim for Stroud to compete with Gloucester and Cirencester in this respect was not realized, and the market did not see the century out.

Lansdown's *pièce de résistance* is undoubtedly the Art School and Museum, a

School of Science and Art, 1910.

building which David Verey described as 'very elaborate Ruskinian Gothic'. It has also been compared with a wedding cake, and is certainly one of Stroud's best-loved buildings.

S.S. Dickinson founded Stroud's first School of Art in 1860. It was then located on the first floor of the old Bedford Arms Inn in High Street. In its first years it had 120 students, and the premises were clearly inadequate, but it was not until a member of the Stanton family made a donation of £1,000 in 1887 that the School of Art was built.

The result was the building in Lansdown of the School of Science and Art. It took over seven years, and was the result of co-operation between J.P. Seddon and a local architect, W.H.C. Fisher. Along its front are displayed in stone medallions the heroes of the applied arts and science of Victorian England, twelve in all, but they do not include the railway engineer Brunel, to whom Stroud owes a greater debt than to those depicted.

Between 1909 and 1954 it housed the Stroud Technical School, and still has the district's Art School. It also became the tightly packed home of the Stroud Museum, launched by a bequest of the property developer William Cowle, who died in 1899. The District Council now proposes to transfer part of the collection to Stratford Mansion.

Relief of Queen Victoria portrayed on the School of Science and Art.

In this direction Stroud had now spread to the boundary of its parish, the Slad stream. On the other side of this was the parish of Painswick, a long strip of that parish stretching down to the river Frome. In the last century the name of this area was Stroudend, and it was for long a rustic retreat of fields and gentlemen's houses.

The oldest of the houses was the Hill, nearer the road to Cainscross than that to Paganhill. An old doorway in the garden pronounces the date of its building 1634, at about the same time as the clothier Thomas Webb also built Rodney House near the church. It was owned by members of the Webb family until 1800, and later was the home of George Holloway's brother, Henry. In modern times it has been extended, and has now a room for functions, an architect's office and a masonic hall.

Several of these houses date from the eighteenth century. The house nearest to Gloucester Street, Willow House, was built about 1800 by Robert Hodges at a time when the road descended steeply to the stream and there were eight or nine steps from the road to his front door. In 1858, it was bought by the county constabulary and acted as the town's police station until the 1960s.

From the 1860s much of Stroudend began to be covered with houses, and

Decorative detail, Stroud Art School, 1890s.

it gained the name of Uplands. Now clearly a suburb of Stroud, the Stroud Board of Health began to look after it in 1885. What David Verey describes as the 'beautiful, unfinished church' of All Saints was built in 1908–10 to the design of the architect, Temple Moore.

This transfer of Uplands from Painswick to Stroud joined the two parts of the old parish of Stroud. Beyond Uplands the ground descended to the Painswick stream, and on the other side was the western piece of Stroud parish, containing the two communities of Paganhill and Whiteshill, the latter notorious until the beginning of the last century because many of its inhabitants spent their time wandering round the countryside begging. This part of Stroud parish also has a scattering of gentlemen's houses like its neighbour.

Looking down on the Painswick stream stands Stratford Mansion, above a pleasant park and pool. The oldest part dates from the seventeenth century, with the house being enlarged over one hundred years later. From 1819 onwards it belonged to Joseph Watts, the proprietor of Stroud brewery. After

Folly Lane, Uplands, 1900.

Uplands, 1935.

Stratford Park Mansion. Built in the seventeenth and eighteenth centuries, it lost its top storey in the twentieth.

the death of Watts' grandson in 1891, for one year it belonged to George Holloway, who is reputed to have installed the first bathroom in the district. A twentieth-century owner removed the top storey of the house, and it was bought by Stroud Urban District Council in 1935.

Between Paganhill and Whiteshill is Farmhill, which had two large houses in the last century. Farmhill House, where George Holloway had previously lived, still stands, its oldest part dating from the seventeenth century. The eighteenth-century house in Farmhill Park was demolished in the 1930s when the estate was divided up for building, though the archway which was the entrance to the drive still stands, to give nearby Archway School its name.

CHAPTER SEVEN

Church and Chapel

Stroud's parish church does not dominate the town. Situated away from the main thoroughfares, its slender spire now dwarfed by the glass-and-concrete pile of the 1960s police station and magistrates' courts, it lies in a backwater.

It began humbly as a chapel in the large parish of Bisley, first mentioned in a document of 1279. By the beginning of the next century two vexed questions had to be settled – how a regular ministry of baptisms and other sacraments was to be maintained in Stroud and who was to pay for the maintenance of the fabric. To settle these an agreement was made before the Archdeacon of Gloucester in 1304, usually known as the Composition. By it a resident chaplain was to live nearby on ground given by the two rectors of Bisley and henceforth known as Pridie's Acre after its then tenant, and the chaplain was to be jointly maintained by the rectors and the people of Stroud. The repairs to the chancel would on this occasion be paid for by the rectors, but in future the inhabitants of Stroud would be responsible for them. The rectors were also to keep rights in Stroud, including the collection of tithes and other fees. For centuries to come Stroud was to be making payments to Bisley church.

In the course of the next hundred years the church acquired a tower and spire, but without benefactors, like those who made splendid the great Cotswold wool churches, it was a small structure, with some additions being made over the years. The last Whittington lord of the manor, Thomas, who died in 1491, probably rebuilt the south aisle, and certainly left instructions that he should be buried there.

Over a century later, in 1610, the manor was bought by Sir Thomas Stephens, Attorney-General to the two sons of James I, Princes Henry and Charles, and after his death in 1613, a local sculptor, Samuel Baldwin, designed the elaborate wall monument still to be seen in the south transept.

Until 1722 the curate of Stroud remained badly paid, making him largely dependent on the contributions of his parishioners. For some time they even had the right to choose new incumbents as those at Painswick had until 1838. In 1722, two rival parties of parishioners chose different candidates, leading to a drawn-out court case. The successful candidate, the Revd Henry Bond, advanced money and secured further grants for the parish from the national

Parish Church from the north about 1910.

fund of Queen Anne's Bounty. Other results of this imbroglio were that the curate now became a perpetual curate with a nominal income of £100, and the bishop acquired the right to be patron.

Even so, those appointed to the living refused to live in Stroud on the grounds that there was no available parsonage. The Revd James Webster became perpetual curate in 1764, but when promoted Archdeacon of Gloucester he held on to the living, having already appointed the Revd William Ellis to act as his stand-in. It was fortunate that Ellis was clearly a man of parts, founding Sunday Schools and a local Reading Society, and the parish does not seem to have suffered unduly from the absence of his superior.

The situation was repeated when the Revd John Seagram was appointed to the parish in 1804, but continued to live in the Wiltshire parish he already held. The following year he made the Revd John Williams his deputy, a position he was to hold until Seagram resigned. Williams lived during most of his curacy in Willow House, the house at Badbrook which was later the police station, and eked out his meagre salary by teaching boys who boarded in his house. He clearly found it difficult to keep up with his duties. On Whit Sunday, 1832, he baptised 113 children in the parish church.

The next year Seagram left, and a petition of Stroud's leading citizens was sent to the bishop seeking Williams' appointment as his successor. However, the bishop refused to agree and appointed the Revd W.F. Powell. Fortunately, Williams had powerful friends, and one of these, Lord Ducie, offered him the living of Woodchester, where he remained vicar until his death in 1857, two years before the birth of his grandson, the poet A.E. Housman, author of *A Shropshire Lad.*

The new vicar of Stroud was the first resident vicar for many years. He only stayed six years here, but in that time took action to remedy some of the existing problems. A vicarage was built in 1838, and the following year Holy Trinity church opened on Stroud Hill with the aim of serving the 'top of town' as a chapel of ease to the parish church. In his old age it was to become the church attended by the Stroud historian, Paul Hawkins Fisher, and his tomb lies in the churchyard.

Incumbent now succeeded incumbent. Dr John Badcock stayed the longest, from 1865 until 1885, and it was during his stay that the church was rebuilt.

There had been many complaints about the state of the old church and its seating arrangements. An 1853 report on the churchyard stated that 'the pestiferous emanations from these receptacles of the dead are polluting the air around us', and in 1854 an order closed it as a burial ground. As to the church itself, the fabric was said to be near collapse, the roof dangerous and the north wall bulging ominously. A parishioner spoke of 'impurities rising from the vaults, immediately under the noses of the congregation'. A further complaint was that the fixed pews in the church were items of property, and such advertisements as this appeared in the local papers:

TO BE SOLD BY AUCTION

At the LAMB INN, STROUD, on Friday, at Four o'clock in the Afternoon,
A LARGE PEW,
capable of containing about ten persons, now in the occupation of
MR. PONTING, butcher, and being one of the best pews in the church.
Stroud Free Press, 16 June 1854.

Because all the pews in the church were private property there was no room for those not owning one. When the Gloucestershire coroner, John Garlick Ball, moved from Minchinhampton to Stroud in 1848, he could find no place in the church for himself and his family, and so attended the Wesleyan chapel. Clearly, something had to be done, but it was delayed.

Parish Church during restoration, 1878.

Parish Church, interior, 1914.

Holy Trinity Church, 1910.

Should the church be rebuilt? Some opposed, wanting to retain as much as possible of the old fabric. A plan to rebuild was frustrated in 1861 because insufficient money was forthcoming, and a further plan based on a design submitted by the leading church architect, Gilbert Scott, was also rejected, on the grounds of expense.

Success came with the arrival of John Badcock. On 8 July 1866, the last service in the old church took place, and for the next two years the congregation met in a tin tabernacle on Slad Road. On 4 August 1868, the new church was consecrated by the Bishop of Gloucester.

The architects were Wilson and Willcox of London and Bath. The new church's appearance has had its critics, David Verey calling it 'a town church which could be anywhere'. However, he was more enthusiastic about the interior, which he compared with a basilica. The most notable contribution to the new building was that of the local carver, Joshua Wall, who designed and executed all the carvings inside and out, including the font and pulpit. The size of the new church was certainly out of scale with the medieval tower and spire, which it was intended eventually to replace.

In title, John Badcock was still perpetual curate, but in 1868 he became a vicar under a new Act of Parliament.

An outstanding native of the town was Father Arthur Stanton, who came

Parish Church, Stanton Memorial Cross, 1915.

from a family of cloth manufacturers. From 1873 to 1913 he was unpaid curate at St Alban's, Holborn, London, and, while there, worked tirelessly among the people of the inner city. In 1912 the Stanton family presented to St Laurence's a wooden screen, and after his death a large wooden cross was added. More recently, in 1989 St Stephen's chapel was created in the north transept as a memorial to him.

Father Stanton was also commemorated elsewhere in the town. In 1916 a mission church dedicated to St Alban was consecrated on the site of the old parish workhouse on Stroud Hill.

On the only occasion that a religious census has been taken in England, in 1851, it showed that the most Nonconformist part of Gloucestershire was the Stroud district. Stroud's leanings go back to the reign of Elizabeth I, when it was reported that the churchwardens objected to practices in church worship, 'idolatry' in church windows, and tombs which they regarded as Catholic.

After the Act of Uniformity of 1661 Dissenters separated from the Church of England, and by 1687 they were holding services in a barn on Stroud Hill. By 1711 a chapel had been built, a building which until well into the nineteenth century was called the Old Meeting. For about one hundred years it was Presbyterian, and then became Congregationalist.

Some of its greatest days came with the arrival in 1811 of the Revd John

John Street Baptist Chapel, 1920.

Burder. He was the driving force behind the forming of new Congregational churches elsewhere in the county and also active in the community generally. We are told that he was involved in more than forty religious and philanthropic societies.

By 1835 his church had more than 200 members including some of the cloth-manufacturing Marling family. It was decided to found a second Congregational chapel, and the site chosen was near the newly-erected Subscription Rooms. The same architect was chosen, the Painswick surveyor, Charles Baker, and the result is generally held to be his best piece of work, called by David Verey 'a splendid classical building'. It was opened in 1837, and Burder's last five years in Stroud were spent as minister there. The Old Chapel on Stroud Hill remained open until 1970, when its congregation joined that of the Bedford Street chapel.

There were several Baptist congregations in the surrounding area, the chapel in the village of King's Stanley proudly proclaiming that it was founded in 1640, but it was not until 1824 that a chapel was built in Stroud in John Street, one of the new thoroughfares of the expanding town.

The eighteenth-century preachers and evangelists, George Whitefield and John Wesley, had strong connections with the town. In 1739 Whitefield, the son of a Gloucester innkeeper, spent a few weeks as curate at Stonehouse in the absence of the vicar, and preached on the bowling-green at Stroud and elsewhere. His leading local follower was Thomas Adams, who built a chapel near his house at Rodborough in about 1766. As Rodborough Tabernacle this became the leading place of worship in Gloucestershire for Whitefield's followers. Although some way out of Stroud it has made a great contribution to the life of the town and district. Of its early preachers, we are told that it was not unusual for them to walk to Bristol on a Saturday evening, preach there and at Kingswood on Sunday, and return on foot 'to the stone quarry or loom' by midday on Monday.

John Wesley's first sermon in Stroud was preached in June 1742, when he addressed his hearers from a butcher's block in the Shambles, an occasion now commemorated by a plaque. In 1763 his followers built a chapel in Acre Street on Stroud Hill. Built in the shape of an octagon, it became known as the 'Round House' and is the oldest surviving Methodist chapel built

Methodist 'Round House', later Salvation Army Citadel, 1905.

St. Rose's Convent, 1935.

originally in that form, though it was extended later. Wesley first preached there in 1765, and did so almost annually until 1790, the year before his death. When about seven years old, the young Paul Hawkins Fisher heard him preach, and remembered him reprimanding some female members of his congregation for taking snuff in the chapel. It now belongs to the Salvation Army, and the Methodists share St Alban's church with the Anglicans.

Other denominations followed. The Primitive Methodists opened their chapel in Parliament Street in 1836, a building which became the theatre of the Cotswold Players after closure of the chapel in the 1950s. In 1852, the Plymouth Brethren founded a meeting-room in Acre Street, which still exists.

Before a Roman Catholic church was built in Stroud, William Leigh, a Catholic convert, had bought in 1846 the Woodchester estate of Lord Ducie, and built a priory church in Woodchester, consecrated in 1849. This was followed in 1853 by the opening of a convent occupied by Dominicans, which became the centre of Catholic activity in the area.

In 1850 another convert, Emily Sandys, turned two rooms of a house she owned in London Road into a chapel for Sunday worship. Later she bought land in Beeches Green, on which a church dedicated to Our Lady of the Immaculate Conception was consecrated in 1857, although the chancel was never built, its site being used for the Rosary School, built in 1883.

St. Rose's Special School, 1935.

From the beginning there was a small community of Dominican nuns associated with the church, and between 1862 and 1867 the convent of St Rose of Lima was built to the design of the Stroud architect, Benjamin Bucknall. The early years of the convent were hard, the sisters maintaining themselves by making ready-made clothing for the Holloways' factory. Bucknall spent the last years of his life in Algiers, and it was from there that he sent back to Stroud the plans for the convent chapel completed in 1895.

Until 1970, the convent ran a secondary school for girls, and in 1912 it opened St Rose's Special School for the physically handicapped, which was at first limited to girls, but more recently has included boys.

CHAPTER EIGHT

Public Bodies and Public Buildings

In 1304 the three manors of Over and Nether Lypiatt and Paganhill had been carved out of the vast parish of Bisley to form what was to become the parish of Stroud. The site of Stroud town was in the area of the manor of Over Lypiatt, and its lords exercised power there. As late as the 1880s the lord of Over Lypiatt received income from the part of Stroud market which was held at the Cross.

Stroud was also situated in the Hundred of Bisley, which contained six other parishes. The lord of the hundred shared power with the lord of the manor at least until the seventeenth century. In 1607 Henry, Lord Danvers who was lord of the hundred won from the king the right to hold markets and fairs in Stroud, and his successors were enjoying income from Stroud's markets and fairs until at least the 1770s.

The local man appointed High Constable of the hundred was responsible for maintaining law and order in the area. By the nineteenth century this office was often held by a Stroud tradesman, and so the druggist James Withey, High Constable from 1823 to 1827, had to deal with the November the Fifth riot of 1824. After the County Police Force was formed in 1839, the High Constable had few duties and the position was superfluous. The last was Thomas Davis, an auctioneer, who held the office between 1845 and 1853, after which no more high constables were appointed.

Such local government as there was in Stroud was for centuries in the hands of the churchwardens and vestry, which consisted of all the householders of the parish. From 1599 onwards their most burdensome duty was providing for the poor. To help them do this, in 1724 they built the parish workhouse on Stroud Hill.

In practice, they came to share power with the so-called Feoffees, a body created in 1636 to administer Pridie's Acre given for the use of the church in 1304, and also other property acquired later. The income received by the Feoffees was divided between the church and the poor.

With the coming of the nineteenth century these arrangements were clearly unsatisfactory. In particular the poor state of Stroud's streets demanded action. The fashion of the day was to set up Improvement Commissions, and Stroud gained one by Act of Parliament in 1825. It was to deal specifically with the town, as its area of activity was limited to within one mile of the parish church. With its members, named in the act, including all the local magistrates it might have been cumbersome in action, but in practice the active Improvement Commissioners were few. Some progress was made, including the paving of the streets and the laying of sewers, but the greatest of the commission's achievements was the lighting of the town by gas in 1833, the gas being provided by the Stroud Gas, Light and Coke Company founded in that year. Otherwise, opposition by the townspeople to the levying of rates was the main obstacle to improvements in the next twenty years.

In 1837, as a result of the new Poor Law, the poor were looked after by the new body of the Board of Guardians of the Poor, and Stroud now acquired a large workhouse, and a register office, where the board met.

In the middle of the century there was general dissatisfaction in the town with sanitary conditions and water supply, leading to an enquiry by a Board of Health Inspector in 1854. After this, the Improvement Commission was replaced by a Local Board of Health with greater powers. Its greatest achievements were the laying down of main sewers in the town and the taking over of the water supply in 1864.

Stroud had depended upon the many wells of the district for its water.

The funeral of the first captain of Stroud's Volunteer Fire Brigade, T.W. Gardner, 29 April 1907.

The old reservoir at the Cross, 1968

From 1769, the Stroud entrepreneur Benjamin Grazebrook had laid down pipes carrying it from Gainey's well on Stroud Hill to a large round basin near the Cross called the Reservoir. From there water was piped to the premises of those Stroud residents in the lower part of the town who paid for it. The upper part of the town was also supplied from other springs on Stroud Hill. The two concerns were combined as the Stroud Water Works Company in 1834.

A major aim of the Board of Health after 1856 was to make sure that all houses were connected to the water supply, and this seems to have been done by 1890.

By the last years of the century the Board of Health in its turn had begun to seem inadequate. It now dealt with a larger area than the Improvement Commission, as Uplands was added to the Stroud urban sanitary district in 1885. In 1894, in its turn the Board of Health was replaced by the Stroud Urban District Council, which was also given wider powers. This proved the longest-lasting local authority of all, only being superseded by the setting up of Stroud District Council in 1974.

The many public buildings of Stroud illustrate its history. First was the Old Town Hall, already mentioned as the Market Hall built at the end of the sixteenth century. Its three top floors were used for other purposes, at the end of the eighteenth century as a school and Sunday school, and as a spinning-house.

The school was that of the so-called Red Boys, founded in 1642 when Thomas Webb, a Stroud clothier, left his house by the churchyard and additional funds to be used by 'two honest poor widows . . . to breed up four poor children'. Two more boys were added by a later charity. They became known as the Red Boys, as their clothing was made of red cloth until well into the nineteenth century. This is an interesting example of the local product, Stroudwater scarlet, being locally used. The boys seem to have had three years' schooling and then an apprenticeship paid for by the charity. Twenty-four of their apprenticeship indentures survive from the years between 1785 and 1812, of which thirteen were to shoe-makers and four to tailors. None was to enter the local cloth industry, in which apprentices were no longer taken.

The schoolmaster also took paying pupils to supplement the fifteen pounds which was his annual salary, and the Red Boys School seems to have reached its peak under Samuel Purnell in the 1760s. Not only were charity boys attending the school but also sons of local squires. Among them was Alexander Ball of Stonehouse Court, during whose school days an event nearly ended his life.

At a time when nearly two hundred crimes were punishable by death, hangings in the county took place at Gloucester and were popular spectacles to which crowds flocked from a fair distance. On one such occasion some Red Boys enacted a hanging themselves with young Ball volunteering to have the noose round his neck. His friends misunderstood his loss of consciousness as acting, and only the intervention of a passing older boy saved his life. He went on to become the captain of a ship in Nelson's fleet at the battle of the Nile, and the governor of Malta.

In 1816–17 the first floor of the Market House was fitted up as a magistrates' court, the school being pushed upstairs into more cramped premises. From 1825 the Improvement Commission, and from 1856 the local Board of Health, held their meetings in what was now called the Town Hall. Big vestry meetings and public meetings were held there, and in 1851 a wing was built on the church side of the building for the local county court. Later still, the Urban District Council used it for offices until it bought more spacious premises at Bank House at the bottom of High Street.

In 1868, the Stroud Volunteer Fire Brigade was established and its fire engine kept at the Old Town Hall. Fires were common in the local mills because of the inflammability of their raw materials. From its foundation its captain was T.W. Gardner, the climax of whose captaincy was attendance at the only review of firemen ever held by Queen Victoria, at Windsor in June 1887.

Stroud's most prominent public building is the Subscription Rooms, a building dominating the town in a way that public buildings rarely do in England. Yet for most of its existence it was run by private bodies, and only came into the hands of the local authority in 1959.

It owes its existence to the creation of Stroud as a parliamentary borough in 1832. Previously, there had been an acute lack of a large public room in the town. In 1831, in order to meet this need Richard Parker had erected the Victoria Rooms in the open space in front of his inn, but the local leaders pushed ahead with other plans as it became clear that Stroud was to become a parliamentary borough.

Four months before the first election in the new borough it was decided to raise money for new public rooms by inviting local people to buy shares of £50 each. Sixty-one shares were bought by fifty-seven people, and a piece of ground purchased at the upper end of George Street which under the name of Hurdle Square had been the scene of the rowdiest meeting in the Reform Bill agitation.

The man of the moment in 1832 was certainly W.H. Hyett of Painswick House, to be triumphantly elected at the head of the poll in the election of that year. Hyett was the brother-in-law of the rising architect, George Basevi, who provided outline plans for the new building. A local surveyor, Charles Baker, of Castle Hale, Painswick, was responsible for supervising the construction. His hand is to be seen in many of the buildings erected in Stroud at this time – the Bedford Street chapel, the union workhouse, the register office and the British school, all but the last of them sharing a common classical style.

When the Subscription Rooms had been nearly completed, building materials were conveyed to the top by means of an inclined wooden walkway which stretched up the building from what is now Threadneedle Street. One Friday, a Woodchester farmer, William Radcliff, after finishing his business had some drinks in the Swan Inn. Somewhat tipsy, he mounted his horse and set off for home. The animal, however, with little direction from its rider found its way on to the inclined walkway and had reached the top before its rider was aware of what had happened. Although assistance was quickly to hand he insisted on backing his mount down the walkway, with the result that it fell and was killed, though he survived.

The new building's main room became the scene of the chief public meetings and entertainments in the town. At one of the first meetings the engineer of the Great Western Railway, Isambard Kingdom Brunel, explained to the local manufacturers the advantages of building a railway through the Stroud valley. In 1846, Messrs Richardson and Sons gave a rock band concert, the instrument consisting of 'a variety of stones in two rows loosely laid upon a couple of straw ropes and struck by stone hammers'. In 1870, Lady Amberley of Rodborough Manor made a speech on women's rights to a Stroud audience for which Queen Victoria said she ought to be whipped.

Other local towns were at first jealous, as the *Gloucester Journal* commented in 1842:

> At Stroud, they have beautiful rooms, built by subscription, for the purposes of the arts and literature as well as of public amusement, whilst nothing of the kind exists either here or at Cheltenham. No artist of talent comes to this county without an invitation to display his powers at Stroud.

On both floors were smaller rooms, and over the years the whole complex has been used for a wide variety of purposes, as it is today, when one room contains the tourist office and others are used for meetings, exhibitions and sales. In 1869, a large porch was added to the front of the Subscription Rooms, under which carriages could unload their passengers, and its roof provided a spacious balcony for the proclamation of monarchs and the declaration of election results.

In front of the Subscription Rooms is a forecourt which has made, and still makes, its contribution to Stroud life. During Stroud August Fair in 1853 the space was occupied by Wombwell's Royal Zoological Collection containing 'unequalled groups of LIONS, TIGERS &c', and after the Crimean War two Russian cannon were presented to the town and remained there until 1940.

In the Second World War an air-raid shelter was built in the open space in front, and now it is the place where local charities set up their stalls.

Near the Subscription Rooms was the Stroud Dispensary, founded before 1755 and the earliest in the county. It was at first financed by subscriptions, legacies and the proceeds of fines, particularly for offences in the cloth industry. After occupying rooms in various buildings in the town, in 1823 it was established in a brick building at the corner of George and Bedford Streets.

In 1835, a casualty hospital was built next to it, the stone building still standing next to the Bedford Street chapel. To it came the victims of local accidents in the mills and on the roads and railways, though only a few patients normally spent more than a couple of hours there. It was staffed by a single resident nurse and visiting surgeon.

By 1872 the number of patients had increased, and a local widow gave £1,000 to the hospital, so starting a fund for a new building. An acre of ground next to Holy Trinity church was given, and a new hospital built and opened in 1875. It cost between £6,000 and £7,000, and had thirty beds. In 1873 the first Hospital Sunday was held. Collections were taken to raise money for it, and later annual Hospital Carnivals were held for the same purpose. It was extended in 1890, and after the First World War a wing was added to celebrate the return of peace.

The first police station in Stroud in 1839 took over the building of the old parish workhouse in Parliament Street, but in 1858 the county constabulary bought Willow House at Badbrook and it was to remain in use as a police station for a century. Alongside it was built at the beginning of this century a magistrates' court.

The fierce political contests of the nineteenth century led to the two parties acquiring premises from which to fight their battles. The Conservative base was Badbrook Hall at the bottom of Gloucester Street, while the Liberals at different times had premises in Gloucester Street and Lansdown. But incomparably the most impressive of these party buildings is Holloway House on one side of the entrance to the station yard. Designed by a local architect, William Clissold, it acted as the Conservative Constituency Office and Club, and as offices for the Holloway Benefit Society. Its foundation stone was laid on August Bank Holiday 1894, when the statue of George Holloway was also unveiled nearby. Two years later it was opened, and described as the best fitted club of its kind in the West of England. It looks like one of the more splendid West End hotels, but no longer serves the purposes for which it was built. The Holloway Society moved to nearby premises in 1934, and after the Second World War the building was taken over by the Red Cross, which occupied it for twenty years. It is now an office block.

Stroud Hospital, 1910.

The oldest building used as a school in Stroud was the Old Town Hall, where the Red Boys were taught until they were transferred to the National School in 1865.

The early Victorian buildings of two schools exist in Stroud. They were built by the rival national educational societies, the National Society aligned with the Church of England and the British Schools Society supported by Nonconformists.

The older is the British School in Slad Road, opened in 1840. To mark the occasion, its 210 pupils walked in procession to the Subscription Rooms to eat dinner. Much later, after a period as a girls' school, the Girls' Central School was started there in the First World War with the name of Badbrook School.

The Black Boy School opened in Castle Street in 1844 as a National School for Girls. The Black Boy, a Jack clock on the front of the Duke of York in Nelson Street, was purchased by public subscription and set up on the front of the school, since which time it has been known as the Black Boy

Old Police Station, formerly Willow House, built about 1800.

Holloway House, 1910, built 1894–6.

The British School, opened 1840.

Black Boy School, opened 1844.

Castle Street Infants School, 1910.

Marling School, 1930.

School. In 1969 it became a teachers' centre. Next door was an infants' school.

Sir Samuel Marling Bt., one of the leading cloth manufacturers of the district and MP for Stroud in 1875–80, had had a long-standing interest in education, being active in the opening of the British School as long ago as 1840. In 1882 he offered £10,000 towards the building of a secondary school for Stroud, and other offers were made to supplement this sum. Marling died the next year, but his family agreed to provide the same amount of money. The Stroud charities also agreed to make funds available to the new school. In 1889, Marling School was opened in Tudor-style buildings on Cainscross Road.

In 1910, Stroud Craft School was founded on a site near Marling School, replacing two schools in Stroud and Brimscombe, when the *Stroud Journal* reported:

> The school is intended for boys between twelve and fourteen years of age, and it is provided with fine workshops and apparatus, in order that the boys may be trained to use their hands and eyes as well as their brains.

Archway, Farmhill Park, which gave its name to Archway School.

In about 1920 it became Stroud Central School, and after 1944 Stroud Technical School, amalgamating with Marling School in 1965.

Marling School provided for local boys, but at the beginning of the century there was still no girls' secondary school. In 1904 a group of local citizens launched the Girls' Endowed School, housed at first at the School of Science and Art in Lansdown. Five years later the Stroud Educational Foundation came into being to administer the two secondary schools and the School of Science and Art in Lansdown. One of its first duties was to erect a new building for Stroud High School, as it was now called, situated also on Cainscross Road near Marling School. The new building was opened by the Duchess of Beaufort in 1912.

In 1926, Stroud Girls' Central School was opened near the boys' school, taking girls from Badbrook School and other local schools. In 1964 it was amalgamated with the High School.

Less than half of Stroud's children enjoyed secondary education until after the Second World War, and it was not until 1961 that Stroud's purpose-built comprehensive school was opened, although its name and position linked it with Stroud history. It was situated on part of the Farm Hill Park estate. In 1834 this had belonged to Henry Wyatt, one of many local people active in the movement for the abolition of slavery in the British Empire led for a long time by William Wilberforce. When this was achieved by Act of Parliament in 1833, he commemorated the occasion by building an archway with an inscription over the entrance to his drive on Farm Hill. The house was demolished in the early 1930s, but the archway survived to give a name and badge to Archway School.

The other educational revolution in recent times has resulted from the building of the Mid-Gloucestershire Technical College on Stratford Road in 1954. Since then, it has experienced forty years of expansion in buildings, courses and numbers of students. It became Stroud College in 1988.

CHAPTER NINE

The Twentieth Century

In the years before the First World War Stroud was a flourishing industrial town, with two breweries and three factories making clothing. Holloway & Co. now also had a factory in Brick Row, and another clothing firm, Williamson, Tratt & Co., after starting in a building near George Street, had built a six-storey brick factory near the railway station. In 1902, Hill, Paul & Co. took this building over, and continued to make clothes there until the 1970s. The third clothing manufacturer was Hound Brand, which had a factory at the corner of Slad Road and Lansdown.

The prosperity of the town encouraged a scheme to establish an electric trolleybus system in the area, but this came to nothing. The old horse buses were replaced by motor buses. The first such service was introduced by the Great Western Railway to convey passengers between Painswick and Stroud.

Various festivities were held at this period. In September 1911 the Mid-Gloucester Historical Pageant of Progress took place in Fromehall Park, when a large number of local people dressed up as historical personages in aid of the funds of the local Liberal party. One result of this pageant was a meeting inaugurating a drama group known as the Cotswold Players, who at first performed all over the county, but who finally settled in Stroud.

In 1913 the Empire Theatre was built on London Road. It opened as a cinema with music hall turns, but also had revues and engaged drama companies.

The First World War began with a series of recruiting meetings and the arrival of Belgian refugees, and ended with the coming of the Australian Flying Corps at Aston Down and Leighterton aerodromes. On 7 June 1918 some of the visiting Australians gave an entertainment, 'While the Billy Boils' in the Subscription Rooms.

In the inter-war period the town benefited from the civic patriotism of several of its inhabitants.

As a small town surrounded by grassy hills, there was little reason for Stroud to participate in the parks movement of the last century. The local commons, and particularly Rodborough Common, were the places for exercise and recreation. All manner of sports were played there, and most Sunday school treats ended with games on the Common. In 1852, there was

Walk to Rodborough Fields, 1905.

a great outcry when it was proposed to enclose Selsley Common, one of its chief opponents, the redoubtable Revd Benjamin Parsons of Ebley, calling the threatened common 'a people's park'. In the twentieth century, there has been a general desire to preserve some of the town's open spaces.

Soon after the First World War a Stroud draper, S.P. Park, presented to the town a piece of land alongside Slad Road in memory of his son and others who had died in the First World War. It became known as the Park Gardens, and the town's war memorial was built at the entrance.

In 1930, when the Urban District Council bought Bank House to provide itself with offices, the garden behind was given to the town by the three sons of Edward Weedon Winterbotham, and provides a pleasant green area below the churchyard in the centre of the town.

Five years later, the council bought Stratford Park, with its lake and fine collection of trees, as a public park and pleasure ground, building an outdoor swimming pool there before the war and a leisure centre after.

Another instance of civic pride was the placing of a clock tower in 1921 at the road junction in front of the Subscription Rooms as a result of a legacy by W.T. Sims, a Stroud grocer. Sims' clock has become a major landmark in the town.

The Second World War had far more impact than the first. It began in September 1939, when a large number of mothers and children were evacuated to Stroud from Birmingham. Thirty-six communal air-raid shelters were installed, each accommodating forty-eight people, and a large shelter, capable of holding seventy, was erected in front of the Subscription Rooms. Fortunately none of these was needed, as no bombs were dropped on the town.

On the other hand, there was a great influx of population. At the peak, it was reckoned that there were over 9,000 extra people in the area, putting great pressure on the town's services. On 16 April 1941 the Minister of Health issued the Lodging Restrictions (Stroud District) Order, making it illegal for visitors in future to stay more than three nights in a house in the area without the consent of the local billeting officer. The order remained in force until almost the end of the war.

Since 1945, some of the main changes have come with the advance of motor transport. There have been new roads, aiming to steer motor transport out of the congested streets in the centre of the town. A widened Merrywalks joins the road to Gloucester and Cheltenham with that to Bath, and Bath Road has been connected with London Road by Dr Newton's Way. A short road, Cornhill, has been built leading from London Road to the Cross, and hence to Bisley. Some of the streets in the centre of the town – High Street and part of Kendrick Street – have been pedestrianized, and most of the others made one-way streets. Multi-storey car-parks have been built in Merrywalks and on London Road. But no one can claim that Stroud's traffic problems have yet been solved.

From the early 1960s a bus station operated on a site in the Merrywalks, but in 1992 a controversial return was made to the system of establishing bus departure points in the town.

Though the area has many industries, Stroud itself has ceased to be an industrial town. Stroud Brewery stopped brewing beer in 1967 and the last of the town's clothing factories closed down in 1990, George Holloway's own firm having ended production in the 1960s. The town has returned to being mainly the service and retail centre for the district.

The most prominent new building in the town is the head office of the Stroud and Swindon Building Society on the site of the old brewery. In its combination of brick and stone, it uses the two materials to be found side by side everywhere in the town. The other main new building in the town, the police station and Magistrates' Courts above the Cross, fits less happily into its setting, reflecting as it does the starkly utilitarian style of the 1960s.

To set against these additions there have been demolitions, mainly in the area of Upper Stroud. The climax came in 1980 with opposition to demolitions of property in the upper High Street in order to build the new road, Cornhill. As a result of an occupation of the threatened buildings by

Park's Drapery at the corner of King & Russell Streets.

Park Gardens, Stroud, 1930.

Sims' clock and Russell Street, *c.* 1950.

militant conservationists a compromise was reached which preserved some of them, including the building identified as a medieval house. A consequence of this episode was the formation of the Stroud Preservation Trust to keep an eye on threatened property and to buy and restore where feasible. A group of interesting buildings has thus been saved, including Withey's shop in High Street and Brunel's railway goods shed.

Stroud became part of the new Stroud District in 1974, and so after eighty years the Urban District Council bowed out. Since 1990 Stroud has had an elected town council of twenty-four, which has sought to make itself a mouthpiece for a town which at times certainly seems to have great need of championship.

Bibliography

Cuss, E. & S.J. Gardiner, *Stroudwater and Thames & Severn Canals in Old Photographs*, Alan Sutton Publishing Limited (1987).

Cuss, E. & S.J. Gardiner, *Stroudwater and Thames & Severn Canals in Old Photographs, A Second Selection*, Alan Sutton Publishing Limited (1993).

Fisher, Paul Hawkins, *Notes and Recollections of Stroud*, 2nd edition, 1891, reprinted Alan Sutton Publishing Limited (1975).

Gardiner, S.J. & L.C. Padin, *Stroud and the Five Valleys in Old Photographs*, Alan Sutton Publishing Limited (1984).

Gardiner, S.J. & L.C. Padin, *Stroud and the Five Valleys in Old Photographs, A Second Selection*, Alan Sutton Publishing Limited (1987).

Gardiner, S.J. & L.C. Padin, *Stroud Road and Rail in Old Photographs,* Alan Sutton Publishing Limited (1987).

Hadfield, C. & A.M. (eds.) *The Cotswolds, a New Study,* David & Charles (1973).

Herbert, N.M. *A History of Stroud, Victoria History of the County of Gloucester,* vol. XI, reprinted (1987).

Hoy, M. & A. *They Met in a Barn, the Story of Congregationalism in Stroud, 1687–1987* (1987).

Libby, John, *Twenty Years' History of Stroud, 1870 to 1890,* Stroud News (1890).

Mann, J. de L., *The Cloth Industry in the West of England from 1640 to 1880,* 1971, reprinted Alan Sutton Publishing Limited (1987).

Sollars, J.C., *The Enquiry which shocked Victorian Stroud,* Stroud Local History Society (1987).

Stroud Museum Association Textiles Group, *The Stroudwater Riots of 1825* (1993).

Symonds, P.R. *'Area Eight' in the war against Hitlerism*, Stroud and Nailsworth Defence Committee (1945).

Tucker, Joan, *Stroud As It Was,* Hendon Publishing (1978).

Tucker, Joan, *Stroud – a Pictorial History,* Phillimore (1991).

Verey, David, *The Buildings of England, Gloucestershire, the Cotswolds*, Penguin (1973).

Walmsley, Philip *The Story of Stroud*, Stroud Local History Society (1993).

Wicks, W.O., *A Desirable Object, the Story of the First 150 years of Stroud Baptist Church*, undated.

The Stroud District and its part in the Great War 1914–1919, Stroud News, undated.

The Victoria History of the Counties of England, a History of the County of Gloucester, vol. XI, *The Hundreds of Bisley and Longtree,* N.M. Herbert (ed.) (1976).

INDEX

Act of Uniformity (1661) 66
Adams, Thomas 68
Air-raid shelter(s) 76, 86
Alderley, Stroud baker 18–20
Algiers 70
Amberley, Lady 75
Apprenticeship 74
Arlingham 1, 11
Art School and Museum *see* School of Science and Art
Arundell family 36
Aston Down aerodrome 84
Aubrey, John 17
Australian Flying Corps 84

Badbrook 37, 77
Badbrook Hall 77
Badcock, Revd Dr John 63, 65
Baker, Charles 67, 75
Baldwin, Samuel 61
Ball, Alexander 74
Ball, John Garlick 63
Ballard, Daniel 38
Banks: County of Gloucester Banking Company 42
  Gloucestershire Banking Company 20
  Grazebrook and Co. 42, 43
  Hollings and Dallaway 21
  Lloyds 42
  NatWest 43
  TSB 20
  Wiltshire and Dorset 43
Bank Gardens 85
Basevi, George 75
Bath 11, 37
Baths 53
Beeches Green 3, 54
Beeching cuts 14
Belgian refugees 84
Berkeley family 47
Birdlip–Lightpill turnpike 37, 42, 43
Birmingham 11, 86
Birt, Joseph 45
Bisley hundred 5, 22, 46, 71
Bisley parish and village 1, 2, 5, 6, 35, 71, 86
Black Boy 21, 78
Bond, Revd Henry 61
The Bowling-Green 37–8, 68
Bowly, Samuel 55
Brand, H.R. 52
Breweries 25, 47–8, 84, 86
Brimscombe 10, 12
Bristol 6, 10, 11, 68
Brunel, Isambard Kingdom 12, 75
Bucknall, Benjamin, printer 40
Bucknall, Benjamin, architect 40, 70
Bull-baiting 28
Burder, Revd John 66–7
Burns, W.G. 38
Buses 84
Bus station 86

Canals: Stroudwater Canal Company/Stroudwater Navigation 6–10, 12, 16, 42
  Thames and Severn Canal 8–10, 16, 42
Cannon, Russian 76
Canton, John 33
Car-parks 86
Casualty Hospital 46, 76
Cemetery 31, 36
Chalford 6, 16, 43
Chambres, Mary 20
Charities: Webb's 25
Charlotte, Queen 37
Chartists 20
Cheltenham 11, 12, 37, 46, 55, 76
Churches and Chapels:
  Acre Street Meeting Room 69
  All Saints', Uplands 58
  Baptist 55, 67
  Bedford Street Congregational 46, 75, 76
  Holy Trinity 34, 35, 36, 63, 65, 76
  Old Chapel Congregational 66–7
  Our Lady of the Immaculate Conception 69
  Primitive Methodist 20, 69
  Rodborough Tabernacle 68
  'Round House', Wesleyan Methodist, later Salvation Army 63, 68–9
  St Alban's, Holborn 66
  St Alban's, Stroud 29, 66, 69
  St Laurence's Parish Church 1, 4, 24, 42, 61-6
  Unitarian 55
  Woodchester Priory 69
Churchwardens 71
Churs (paths linking streets in Upper Stroud) 18
Cirencester 1, 11, 55
Clissold, William 77
Cloth-hall 52
Clothing industry: Hill, Paul & Co. 84
  Holloways' 49, 50, 53, 70, 84, 86
  Hound Brand 84
  Williamson, Tratt & Co. 84
Civil War, 1642–9, 5
Codrington, C.W. 46
Composition of 1304 61, 71
Convent of St Rose of Lima 70
Corn Exchange 23
Cotswold Players 69, 84
Cottage Building Society 50
Cowle, William 36, 56
Crew, William 25
Cricket 50
Crimean War 76
the Cross 6, 24, 26-8, 86

Dallaway, James 21
Danvers, Henry, Baronet 5, 71
Davis, Thomas 71
Defoe, Daniel 6
Delmont, Lieutenant Joseph 40, 42
Deodand (piece of property, which, having caused death of person, was forfeit) 42
Dickens, Charles 40
Dickinson, Sebastian Stewart 51, 53
Dispensary 76
Dissenters 66
Dominicans 69, 70
Dorington, Sir John, Baronet 33, 50, 51
Ducie, Lord 63, 69
Dudbridge 10, 15
Dursley 52

Ebley 85
Ebley Mill 7
Elections: 1834 E. Gloucestershire 45–6
  1852 Stroud 15
  1874–5 Stroud 51-2
  1880 Stroud 52
  1885 Stroud 52
  1886 Mid-Gloucestershire 52
  1886 Mid-Gloucestershire 52
Ellis, Revd William 62
Empire Theatre 84

Face, Susan Dancey 31
Fairs 5, 21, 38, 71, 76
Field estate 36
First World War, 1914–18, 84
Fisher, Paul Hawkins 11, 17-18, 24, 34, 35, 36, 40, 63, 69
Fisher, W.H.C. 56
Framilode 1, 7, 11
Freebury, Charles 43
Frome river 1, 6, 7, 8
Fromehall Park 84

Gainey's Well 73
Gardner, T.W. 74
Gardner, Thomas 38
Gas-lighting 47, 72
George III 37
Gladstone, W.E. 51
Gloucester 1, 6, 11, 14, 16, 25, 55, 67, 74
Gloucestershire Repository 17, 40, 44
Grazebrook, Benjamin 73

Grazebrook, Joseph 42
Guard-house 28

Harmer, F.W. 40
Harrison, Charles 43
Havelock, Sir Henry, Baronet, VC 51
High Constable Bisley Hundred 22, 71
Hodges, Charles 44
Hodges, Robert 57
Hollings, John 20, 21
Holloway, George 36, 49–53, 60, 77
Holloway, Henry 49, 57
Holloway House 77, 79
Holloway Society 49–50, 77
Hopson, William 53
Horns Valley 36
Horsley 5
Hospital 34, 36, 76, 77
Hospital Carnival 76
Hospital Sunday 76
Houses: Bank House 18–20, 74, 85
  Brownshill Court 53
  the Castle 33, 35
  Farmhill House 60
  Farmhill Park 60, 83
  Godolphin House 32
  the Grange 42
  the Hill 57
  Medieval house 4 ,88
  Rodney House 24, 25, 57
  Rowcroft House 42, 43
  Stratford Park (Mansion) 47, 56, 59–60
  Wellington Place 44
  Willow House 57, 62, 77, 78
Housman, A.E. 63
Hughes, Robert 25
Hurdle Square 75
Hyett, W.H. 53, 75

Imperial Hotel 13
Inns: Anchor, Wallbridge 10
  Bear, Rodborough 6
  Bedford Arms (first site) 20, 56
  Butcher's Arms, Shambles 23
  Chequers, King Street 37, 53
  Corn Hall Hotel, Shambles 23
  Duke of York, Nelson Street 78
  George, High Street 11, 25, 32, 37
  Golden Heart, King Street 11, 37–8, 53
  Green Dragon 38
  Horse Shoes, Nelson Street 32
  King's Arms, King Street 37, 38
  Lamb, Church Street 11, 63
  Marlborough Head, High Street 20
  New George, Nelson Street 32
  Royal George, King Street 11, 26, 37, 38–43, 45, 46
  Ship, Wallbridge 10
  Sun-dial, London Road 44, 45
  White Hart, the Cross 45
  Swan, Union Street 11, 26, 75

Jenner, Miss 21
Jewish synagogue 55
Johns, Revd William 32

Kean, Edmund 20
Keene's workshop 20
Kendrick, Charles 43
Kendrick, Charles Freebury 44
Kendrick's Orchard 43, 44, 53
King's Stanley 5, 67
Kingswood 68
The Knapp 32
Knight, William 22

Lansdown Hall 51, 55
Lawrence, William 12–13
Leighterton aerodrome 84
Leonard Stanley 5
Leigh, William 69
Libby, John 52
Library 51, 55
Lodging Restrictions Order (1941) 86
Little Mill 53
London 1, 11, 33, 42
Loyal Stroud Volunteers 42

Magistrates' Court 74
Mansfield, Edward 55
Market 5, 20, 23, 24, 26, 27, 55, 71
Market House *see* Old Town Hall
Marling family 67, 81
Marling, Sir Samuel Stephens, Baronet 52, 81
Mid-Gloucester Historical Pageant of Progress 84
Mid-Gloucestershire constituency 52
Mid-Gloucestershire Technical College 83
Miles, John 21
Minchinhampton 1, 2, 5, 63
Minchinhampton Common 1,
Minister of Health 86
Moore, Temple 58
Mutual Provident Benefit Society 50

Nailsworth 15
Napoleonic War 40
National Society 78
Nether Lypiatt 4, 71
Newspapers: *Gloucester Journal* 14, 38, 40, 47, 76
  Gloucestershire Chronicle 46
  Monthly Observer 40
  Morning Chronicle 40
  Stroud Free Press 11, 40, 63
  Stroud Journal 40, 50, 52, 55
  Stroud News 40, 50, 53, 55, 82
  Stroud News & Journal 55
Norton, John 15

Old Town Hall 7, 23, 73-4, 78
Over Lypiatt 4, 5, 23, 71
Oxford University Botanic Garden 5

Paganhill 4, 58, 71
Paine, Dr William Henry 25, 53–5
Painswick 1, 42, 57, 61, 84
Painswick stream 1
Park, S.P. 85
Park Gardens 85, 87
Parker, Richard 45, 75
Parsons, Revd Benjamin 85
Paul, Sir George Onesiphorus 10
Pearce, Hugh 52
Piccadilly Mill 35
Pillory 28
Pitching 24
Police 71
Police station 29, 57, 61, 77, 78
Ponting, Mr, butcher 63
Poole, Thomas 29
Poor relief 71
Post Office 21
Powell, Revd W.F. 63
Pridie's Acre 23, 24, 61, 71
Pugin, A.W.N. 40
Purcell family 37
Purnell, Samuel 74

Queen Anne's Bounty 62

Radcliff, William 75
Railcar service 15–16
Railways: Bristol and Gloucester 14
  Cheltenham and Great Western Union 12
  Gloucester & Cheltenham 12
  Great Western 12–16, 47, 75, 84
  Midland 10, 14, 15, 16
Reading Society 62
Red Cross 77
Reform Acts, First (1832), 43, 46, 75
  Second (1867), 50–51
Register Office 72, 75
Reservoir 73
Richardson, Messrs & Sons 75
Riots: Guy Fawkes 1824 22
  1834 Election 45–6
Roads 1, 6, 11, 12, 13
Rock band concert 75
Rodborough 2

Rodborough Common 1, 6, 84
Rodborough Fort 50
Rodborough Manor 75
Romieu, Mrs 33
Rowcroft 13, 37, 42-3
Russell, Lord John 38, 40, 43

Salisbury 21
Salmon Springs 47
Sandys, Emily 69
Sapperton 10, 13
School of Science and Art 55–8, 82
Schools: Archway 60, 82, 83
  British 75, 78, 79, 81
  Castle Street Infants 80, 81
  Charity 32
  Girls' Endowed 82
  Girls' Central 78, 82
  Miss Jenner's 21
  Marling 81
  National (Black Boy) 21, 22, 78, 80
  Red Boys 74, 78
  Mrs Romieu's 33
  Rosary 69
  St Rose's Convent 70
  St Rose's Special 70
  School of Art 55–6
  Stroud Borough 55
  Stroud Central 82
  Stroud Craft 81
  Stroud Grammar School 55
  Stroud High 82
  Stroud Technical 56, 82
Scott, Gilbert 65
Seagram, Revd John 62
Second World War, 1939–45 30, 76, 77, 83, 85–6
Seddon, J.P. 56
Selsley Common 85
Sergeaunt, Lieutenant 42
Shambles 7, 22–4, 26, 68
Shops: Co-op 28
  Moonflower 22
  Park's Drapery 87
  Timpson's 45
Siddons, Sarah 33
Sims, John 25
Sims, W.T. 85
Sims' clock 85, 88
Singer, Isaac 49
Slad stream 1, 6, 53, 57
Slad valley 11
Slavery, campaign against 45, 83
Spear, bank-robber 21
Stage-coaches 11
Stanton family 56
Stanton, Father Arthur 65–6
Stanton, A.J. 51
Stanton, W.H., MP 38
Stanton, W.J. 51
Stephens, Sir Thomas 61
Stocks 28
Stonehouse 14, 15, 67
Stow-on-the-Wold 18
Stratford Park 85

Streets: Acre Street 68
  Badbrook Lane 53
  Bath Place 44
  Bath Terrace 13, 44
  Bedford Street 20, 21, 76
  Bisley Road 31, 35–6,
  Brick Row 84
  Castle Street 21, 78
  Chapel Street 18
  Church Street 11, 24–5
  Cornhill 26, 86
  Dr Newton's Way 86
  Folly Lane, Uplands 59
  (Great) George Street 44, 76, 84
  Gloucester Street 6, 53, 77
  High Street 4, 6, 11, 18–22, 38, 40, 53, 56, 86
  Hollow Lane 35
  Horns Road 35, 36
  John Street 67
  Kendrick Street 21, 52–3, 86
  King Street 11, 26, 37–41, 87
  Lamb Lane 25
  Lansdown 51–3, 55–6, 77, 84
  London Road 44, 53, 84, 86
  Lower Street 18, 30
  Merrywalks 86
  Middle Street 18, 33
  Nelson Street 26, 31–3, 78
  Old Bisley Road 32
  Parliament Street 26, 31, 77
  Russell Street 41, 44, 87, 88
  Slad Road 54, 65, 78, 84, 85
  Stratford Road 83
  Threadneedle Street 49, 53
  Union Street 11, 25–6
Stroud and Swindon Building Society 86
Stroud Board of Guardians 29–30, 72
Stroud Board of Health 58, 72–3, 74
Stroud College 83
Stroud District (Cowle) Museum 56
Stroud Educational Foundation 82
Stroud Feoffees 24, 26
Stroud Galley Company 10, 71
Stroud Improvement Commission 20, 22, 28, 71–2, 74
Stroud Mutual Improvement Society 53
Stroud Parish 71
Stroud Preservation Trust 22, 88
Stroud Town Council 88
Stroud Urban District Council 20, 55–6, 73, 74, 85, 88
Stroud Volunteer Fire Brigade 74
Stroud Hill 6, 17, 29
Stroudend *see* Uplands
Stroud Water Works Company 73
Stroudwater 6, 17

Stroudwater Flying Coach 11
Subscription Rooms 45, 46, 67, 74–6, 78, 84, 85
Sunday schools 62, 85

Temperance Hall *see* Lansdown Hall
Teachers' Centre 21
Theatre 20, 25, 69
Thornton, Edward 42
Throckmorton, John 5, 23
Tourist Office 76
Trollope, Anthony 29
Trows, Severn 10

Uplands 57–9

Vans, Jamie 28
Verey, David 23, 29, 56, 58, 65, 67
Vestry 71
Victoria, Queen 14, 57, 74, 76
Victoria's Golden Jubilee 55
Victoria Rooms (Buildings) 41, 75
Vincent, Henry 38

Wakefield family 38, 40
Wall, Joshua 65
Wall, Thomas 11, 37
Wallbridge 6, 8, 10, 26, 37, 42
War memorial 85
Water supply 28, 72–3
Watts, Joseph 47, 58, 60
Webb, Thomas 25, 57, 74
Webster, Revd James 62
Wesley, John 31, 67–9
Whitefield, George 37–8, 67–8
Whitehall 33, 35, 67
Whiteshill 58
Whittington family 4
Whittington, Richard 4
Whittington, Thomas 61
Whitworth, Robert 10
Wilberforce, William 83
Williams, Revd John 62–3
Wilson and Willcox 65
Winterbotham family 20
Winterbotham, Edward Weedon 85
Winterbotham, Revd W.E. 20
Winterbotham, Strachan and Playne 20
Withey family 22
Withey, James 22, 71
Wolfe, James 32
Wombwell's Zoological Collection 76
Woollen cloth manufacture 1, 4, 6, 74
Woodchester 37, 75
Woodchester Park 40, 69
Workhouses 29, 36, 71, 75
Wotton-under-Edge 52
Wyatt, Henry 83
Wye family 4, 5